W9-DCD-614

The Heart
To Forgive

To Hansy — my life story!
Enjoy reading my life story!
Much love, light & laughter

Alin 6/21/08

The Heart To Forgive

✦

Reclaiming Our Relationship after Infidelity

MIMI GABRIEL

with the collaboration of Les Gabriel

iUniverse, Inc.

New York Lincoln Shanghai

The Heart To Forgive
Reclaiming Our Relationship after Infidelity

Copyright © 2007, 2008 by Mireille Gabriel

All rights reserved. No part of this book may be used or reproduced by any means, graphic, electronic, or mechanical, including photocopying, recording, taping or by any information storage retrieval system without the written permission of the publisher except in the case of brief quotations embodied in critical articles and reviews.

iUniverse books may be ordered through booksellers or by contacting:

iUniverse
2021 Pine Lake Road, Suite 100
Lincoln, NE 68512
www.iuniverse.com
1-800-Authors (1-800-288-4677)

Because of the dynamic nature of the Internet, any Web addresses or links contained in this book may have changed since publication and may no longer be valid.

The views expressed in this work are solely those of the author and do not necessarily reflect the views of the publisher, and the publisher hereby disclaims any responsibility for them.

A portion of the proceeds from the sale of every copy of *The Heart to Forgive* is donated to Haitian charities.

ISBN: 978-0-595-44286-7 (pbk)
ISBN: 978-0-595-69365-8 (cloth)
ISBN: 978-0-595-88615-9 (ebk)

Printed in the United States of America

Possessiveness always ends by destroying what it tries to protect.

Absolute control over another human being is neither possible nor desirable.

It is only natural to want to share ourselves intimately ... it only becomes a problem when we need it to become an exclusive, full-time arrangement.

It should be a relief rather than a threat to find that those we love have a capacity for loving others as well as being loved.

We really are capable of loving many people at the same time without diluting what we have to give.

The more loving experiences we have, the more we have to bring with us when we focus on a deep, intimate relationship.

The quality of love is not strained when it is shared; rather it is intensified and most assuredly improves with the experience.

Leo Buscaglia—Born for Love

This book is for those who know love, the one thing that truly matters.

TABLE OF CONTENTS

Acknowledgements

There are several people I want to thank. This book would not have been written if it weren't for the role they played in my life. I tend to categorize rather than prioritize, and there is no particular order in which the people I'd like to acknowledge are listed.

I owe a great deal to several mentors, speakers, authors, and I thank in particular Marianne Williamson, Reverend Michael Beckwith, Wayne Dyer, Anthony Robbins, Jim Rohn and Brian Tracy. Their powerful teachings have been a constant source of strength. The numerous seminars I attended with them as well as their recorded messages and written works have provided me with invaluable tools to help me along the way. I have listed some of the books and programs I've most benefited from at the end of this book.

Our daughters Nathalie, Melissa and Tanya have been extremely supportive during the frequent discussions that would eventually give me clarity about what exactly I wanted to accomplish. Was I writing to heal my heart and vent my frustrations, or to inspire others and help them heal their own wounds? Ultimately, it was for all these reasons. The book took a form of its own when my own healing was nearing completion, and I surrendered entirely to a Higher Power. That is when forgiveness became the central point. It cannot be easy for our daughters to face our intimate life displayed so publicly, and I thank them deeply for their courage and tolerance as well as their forgiveness!

My dear friend and Life Coach Mary Allen, as well as all the *Joyful Achievers* with whom I spent an entire year sharing from the heart at our boot camp helped me get clarity during one of the most trying years of my life. Thank you all for the laughter, the light and the love!

My utmost gratitude to my Tony Robbins crew pals, in particular the multi-talented and loving Ann "Can-Do" MacIndoo, Margaret Irving, the Energy Rocket, Carol Grove, Elizabeth Vargas, Judy Osuna, Amie Lee Marks and Linda Kedy, and of course our fearless leader Loren Slocum and her husband Shore Slocum who always offered me the best advice: 'Follow your heart!' I'm also grateful to Merrily Heck whom I met at a Date with Destiny event and who positively impacted my destiny. A gifted healer, Merrily was the first to introduce me to the benefits of meditation.

Huge thanks to Ed Montgomery from your spiritual Goddess (!) for the encouragement to stay with the project; to Adam Fitzgerald who shared priceless insights on the male psyche with me; and to Miguel Diaz, 'my bodyguard' for helping me understand the Venezuelan culture.

I'm deeply grateful to many dear friends who allowed me to empty my heart, grieved with me and laughed with me: Raven and Paul, Donna and Stephan, Yvonne and Troy, Judith and Reginald, Deanna and Rick, Maria and Ted, Sarah, Corinne, Michelle, Elena, Emiliana, Alex, Estella, Diana … even if some of you live continents away, I hold you close to my heart.

I treasure my friendship with Adelle Stone, Bethsy San Millan and Leila Carr and I truly appreciate their editorial advice as well! Bethsy San Millan in particular took the project at heart and was relentless in her revisions.

I've always been inspired by Oprah Winfrey and, in part, I owe it to her to have persevered with this book, remained authentic, and lived up to a part of my life's purpose, which is to help others improve the quality of their relationships.

My editor Steve Roche first organized the book from a pile of journal entries and numerous e-mails. He candidly asked me one day: "So, is the story nothing more than two people who are in love, experience infidelity and learn to forgive?" Considering that in Europe, where he lives, infidelity is not as taboo as in the United States, he was puzzled by the book's subject. Neither one of us had any idea how the story would unfold.

Last and foremost, I thank my best friend, my first and only love, my life-long partner and the best lover I could ever dream of, my husband Les, who is demonstrating one more time his deep love for me by supporting me in this project. He patiently listened while I read entire chapters of the book, during several road trips from Houston to Austin to visit our grandbaby. He reviewed the chapters written in his name, eliminating what he deemed superfluous. He even offered his private journals to shed some light on specific events. His collaboration is greatly appreciated. He is a very private man and this is as public as it gets! It's a good thing that he too has *the heart to forgive!*

Mimi Gabriel
Maui, Hawaii
July 17, 2007

Preface

Writing about something as personal as an extramarital love affair is easy when it is in your journals and intended for your eyes only. Very often I wrote in my native French, in case my writings fell in the wrong hands. How then did I get to the point when I decided that I should make the story public? There clearly was a need. I couldn't find a book that dealt with the situation my husband and I were facing. When I participated in a Possibility Conference, back in January 2002, I listened to Michael Beckwith, Wayne Dyer, Bob Proctor and Larry Wilson over several days and the recurring message from them all was: "You do not want to die with your music still inside of you." I had begun writing the notes to my musical piece. Their message was instrumental in my decision to share it with the world. This book is written from the heart, with the hope that it will help others heal as it has helped my husband and me.

When I gathered journal entries and e-mails exchanged over a period of a few months, there was enough to fill several pages, a few chapters even. But there was no end in sight for the ongoing saga! That is why it took seven years to complete the manuscript! At times I asked myself: is writing the book what helps me be more forgiving or is it forgiveness that enables me to write the story? In the end, it was a combination of both.

I have changed the names of most of the characters to protect their identity. Although written as a novel, this is a true story. It is based on real events in my life, and incidents that happened to people I know. The chapters written from the viewpoint of other characters are based on letters written to me, or from personal conversations. If the dialogues are not exactly as they occurred, it is because they are written from memory.

I was fortunate to have attended countless self-improvement seminars over the years prior to facing the situation my husband and I dealt with. The teachings of masters and mentors in the field of personal development greatly contributed to my ability to face our circumstances. I had acquired the necessary tools thanks to an insatiable thirst for knowledge about human behavior. That thirst stemmed from an early exposure: when I was growing up in Port-au-Prince Haiti, my boyfriend gave me a 1250-page long volume called *Les Prodigieuses Victoires de la Psychologie et les Triomphes de la Psychanalyse* by Pierre Daco. Although I was only fifteen or sixteen years old at the time, I consulted this book often. It fascinated me. Several years later, when I was introduced to cassette programs by Leo Buscaglia, Earl Nightingale, Brian Tracy, Dennis Waitley, Lou Tice, Bob Mowad and many other experts in the field of psychology, I would listen to them over and over, learning as much as I could. This exposure to psycho-analysis and personal achievement enabled me to cope more effectively with our crisis.

If a few marriages are saved because of our story, if you, or a friend, a parent, or a child benefit from our experience, I will be grateful. Words spoken are often quickly forgotten. Words written have a longer-lasting impact. The Heart to Forgive is part of my legacy.

1

The confession

The minute I saw him I knew something was not quite right. My husband, Jean Paul, seemed aloof, distant and barely made eye contact when he caught sight of me at the San Francisco Airport.

For the past several months he had been working on an overseas project in Venezuela on three to four week stints. The frequent separations had started to take their toll. He half-heartedly hugged and kissed me. Was he going through a midlife crisis? My response was passionless. This was the man I had been with for more than three decades. I knew Jean-Paul well. I wondered if he too was feeling the same heaviness in his chest, the same apprehension, some sort of premonition that something was terribly wrong.

We were attending a seminar in San Francisco and were sharing a small apartment with my brother and our daughters Chloe and Danielle. Our middle daughter, Suzanna hadn't been able to free herself from her summer job at Penn State. The sleeping arrangement didn't provide much privacy, but that alone could not explain the coldness I felt creeping between us throughout our stay.

An in-depth discussion about what was going on would have to wait, though, since after the seminar Jean Paul left for a 10-day vacation with his brother in Maui.

Chloe went back to her life in Alaska and Danielle returned home to Dallas with me.

Perhaps Jean-Paul was preoccupied with the most frequent cause of our arguments: our finances. Maybe he wanted me to get a job. It had been a recurring theme: I was spending too much money. He was sacrificing by having to work overseas. He had even mentioned that we should sell our home and get a smaller one. I had ignored him since it had been only three years since we had this gorgeous home custom-built for us. And I believed there was no reason to cut down on expenses, or for me to work outside of home. I had contracted a landscaper while he was gone to have new flowerbeds and I had ordered some fruit bearing trees for the backyard. I bought fresh flowers for our bedroom and our living area. The yard was looking great. The house was welcoming. I wondered how Jean-Paul would react!

Picking him up from Dallas-Fort Worth Airport the following Wednesday, I felt that the distance between us was turning into a crevasse.

Standing over six feet tall with handsome features and graying hair, Jean-Paul cut an impressive figure. He had kept himself in good shape over the years by cycling almost every day. He had smiling eyes, a great sense of humor and a very generous heart.

He didn't look so good when he came through the gate at Arrivals, though. He looked every bit his age. There was tightness in his jaw which always indicated the intensity of his thoughts, and the swollen vein on his temple was sending distressing signals. My husband didn't utter a single word that day about what was bothering him. Nor did he touch me in an affectionate way. He made no comments about the new landscaping or the flower arrangements, which caused my suspicion that our relationship had suffered a major blow to deepen.

It took a few days before anything was said. Neither one of us attempted to talk about the heaviness that was engulfing us until Friday night.

As we laid next to one another in bed I could not hold back for any longer.

"Okay, are you going to tell me what's on your mind?"

"There's nothing."

"Come on, I know that something is troubling you."

I asked him repeatedly, but each time he denied it with a different answer.

He said he was hot, that he had just been away to Hawaii and was suffering from jetlag; that he had been on a diet and lost 14 pounds; that he was tired, that he had eaten too much rich food and was uncomfortable ...

I insisted: "Jean-Paul, I really would like to know what happened in Venezuela."

"There's nothing to say."

I went for it: "Oh yes, there is. I'd like to know her name and what she looks like."

"What are you talking about?"

For a fleeting moment I had a tiny hope that this was all my imagination playing tricks with me. But deep inside a woman knows. So I pushed on with my questions.

"You can tell me. Talk to me, the friend, not to the wife."

There was a long pause followed by a lengthy and loud sigh. I remained as quiet as a mouse. It was dark and Jean-Paul couldn't possibly have seen the look of curiosity mixed with terrified apprehension on my face. Finally after what seemed like a very long time, he spoke:

"Am I so transparent?"

There, it was. My suspicions were confirmed. He was going to confess fully but I felt like I needed to say something first.

"Baby, you've been back for three days and we still haven't made love. That is a definite clue!"

"Okay, okay."

Jean-Paul let out another long sigh.

"I wanted to wait until we went to Kona next month to tell you. The reason I haven't been intimate with you is that I've met someone else."

Did he say Kona? That meant that he was still planning to attend the seminar I would be staffing in Hawaii. Good. That was good. I knew how life-altering these seminars could be. Jean-Paul would benefit from the segment on relationship especially. Wait … what else did he say? He met someone else?

I felt a huge stabbing pain in my upper chest. I thought back to a healing workshop with a therapist the year before. Marianna had taught the group to detach from a situation and to protect our energies by 'cutting the cord'. I ordered myself to do just that but my heart continued to pound out of control. Cut, cut, cut. The energy cords that attached me to my husband and to the situation he was revealing to me needed to be cut before I could hear anything else. My hand was a sword, the cords were stacked together in my left hand and I mentally cut, cut, cut … That should work! Keep cool, I thought, maybe he's just making it up. He is teasing you. He is going to tell you it's a joke. Relax! It's a farce! Your husband is a big joker …

"I feel it would not be fair to her to be with you because it's really her I want to be with," Jean-Paul said before I had a chance to ask him whether or not he was kidding.

No, he can't be saying this. I must be hallucinating. God, tell me this is not happening!

Jean-Paul continued: "I've known her for about a year now."

Had it really been a year since he had started going to Venezuela? It was worse than I had feared. Remain calm. Do not start crying. By all means, control those tears.

In a low, barely audible voice I asked: "So, what does she look like? I suppose she's beautiful and very successful, right?"

"Not really. She's … she's a secretary. She's my secretary."

"What's her name?"

"Efelia."

All I could manage was: "Is she pretty?"

"No, not really. Pleasant looking. Not pretty."

Why is it that men have to fall in love with their secretaries? It must be the awe and admiration these young demoiselles have for their bosses. The look of adoration they use when their eyes meet. This one must be completely dazzled by the mature, secure, handsome and successful man who has now fallen into her net.

"So … is she young?"

"34."

"So she could be your daughter!"

"Come on!"

"Come on what? You're 52 so you could have been a father at 18!"

"Are you sure you want me to tell you more?"

I bit my tongue. "Keep quiet if you want him to confide in you," I told myself. My "emotional shield" was in place, though. Didn't I learn that one can surround oneself with this virtual plexi-glass cage and let sight and sound come through but not any emotional upset? Let me try it right now: are my emotions being kept under control by the shield? Are they hitting it and rebounding, without penetrating it, without hurting me? I have learned this technique. I have encouraged others to use it. It should work. It's just taking a little longer than expected.

I didn't want to see his face. I didn't want to feel his touch. That would have been too hard. The shield would protect me from becoming too vulnerable. My thoughts were racing. I wondered if I was only getting what I deserved for having been such a nagging wife. I'd also been quite content with him being away so much as it had given me such valued freedom. Plus, I had been praying for something to happen to our relationship so that it could improve or take a different turn. It was turning all right. Maybe not in the direction I'd been hoping for but it sure was taking a turn.

Jean-Paul broke me out of my thought pattern:

"She has had so much tragedy in her life but, believe me, it's not pity that makes me want to be with her. What started as a simple friendship has evolved, and this whole thing only took place a couple of weeks before I left Caracas."

I could hear the wind outside our bedroom door leading to the patio. It was a typical Texas summer night: warm yet breezy, which is always a welcome relief after the intense heat of the day. I could also hear Jean-Paul's heavy breathing. His pauses between statements were long. I remained quiet, too shocked to react.

He started stroking my hair but I felt disconnected and resolved not to shed any tears.

"I want you to know that I did not mean for this to happen. It is the first time since I've known you that I feel the way I do toward another woman."

There were more long pauses and deep sighs. I could take this. Hadn't I been there myself? It didn't seem like so long ago that I had fallen madly in love with someone else during our marriage.

My reverie was interrupted:

"There are many beautiful women in Venezuela but none were ever able to get my interest until I met her. I found a soul mate. She's got a good heart, she's very loving, very giving and totally selfless. Maybe she reminds me a little of my mother. I just enjoy being loved and giving her love."

Did he really have to turn the knife inside my wound? By now, I felt like I'd heard enough as it sounded really serious but I decided to pretend with every ounce of energy I possessed that I was strong. I chose to ignore the fact that he'd said she was a soul mate. He and I were soul mates. We had been soul mates forever. As a young teenage girl growing up in Haiti, as a testament of my love for him, I used to write his name inside a heart on my sneakers. It was meant for all my classmates to see on gym days, to the horror of Mother Marie Anne, one of the nuns at my school, *Pension-*

nat Ste Rose de Lima also known as Lalue. That girl wasn't even born when Jean-Paul and I first fell in love! She could not be stepping into our lives and invade it so easily. I maintained the façade of the understanding wife so that he could go on and empty his soul. I remained as quiet as I could, allowing his words to clobber me relentlessly.

I was somewhat disappointed that he hadn't chosen someone gorgeous and successful. I might have felt better about myself if my rival was of a higher caliber. But instead he'd chosen a defenseless, single mother of a young boy whose middle name was also our family name. How ironic was that?

Jean-Paul went on to tell me about all the tragedies this girl had to face in life. Her father had committed suicide, her boyfriend had died of a heart attack and another man she met got her pregnant and then went off to marry someone else. It was obvious that Jean-Paul felt pity for her. I decided he was confusing that with love.

"When you hear of so much pain in someone's life, you can't help but ask yourself: Where was I when she needed help?" Jean-Paul continued. "Why couldn't I have been there for her?"

I stopped him right there: "What are you talking about? You were with me, where you were supposed to be! Has she given you some 'dlo sott' (stupid water) to drink? Goodness gracious, this is her story. Not yours."

Dlo sot? That was what crafty women used to weave spells around a male they could not otherwise attract by themselves. It was very common in our Haitian culture to hear of people being given weird potions that made them lose their willpower. I decided that Jean-Paul was undoubtedly under such a spell. I needed to say something:

"Remember what we've learned: when someone tells us his or her story: we should not get into it. You must protect yourself and you must separate yourself from other people's tragedies. You need to put a shield around you to protect your energy field. Otherwise, you'll just get sucked right into their problems."

Jean-Paul didn't respond. He was obviously deep into her story already. I, however, could feel neither pity nor sympathy.

I found the strength to ask: "On a scale of one to ten, how do you feel about her?"

"Eleven."

"And the way you feel about me?"

"Nine."

Why did I ask if I didn't want to hear the answer? At least he was being honest, even though it was hurtful.

"What do you want to do?"

"I want to love her."

He cannot be saying this. Doesn't he realize how hurtful that is?

"If you had known that you would not be returning to Caracas for further assignments would you have let yourself fall in love with her?"

"Yes." He didn't hesitate.

"So do you want us to separate? Do you think we should get a divorce? You can't keep both a wife and a mistress."

"I really haven't thought that far ahead. This just happened."

"Well maybe we should go to a marriage counselor."

My words were dictated by past references to other people's stories about the breakup of their relationships. I was supposed to be the expert in that field. I was the one who helped other people deal with the blows that life dealt them. What did I teach the women I spoke to at the Fort Worth shelter? "Don't ever let anyone's actions, no matter how hurtful they are, dictate how you live the rest of your life." Didn't my friends always come to me for advice? I needed those tools NOW to help me out of this nightmare.

Disbelief and denial were quickly being replaced by a sense of betrayal and unbearable grief.

Jean-Paul cut in by reminding me about an affair of the heart I'd had ten years previously:

"Now you know how I felt when you told me you were in love with Adam."

At the time, I thought that the love I felt for Adam would be eternal. I thought we were soul mates and I fantasized that he might want me to leave my husband to be with him. I had let myself fall in love with him. The feelings had since completely evaporated. Was my husband suggesting that his romance faced a similar fate?

I forced myself to remain centered and sane but Jean-Paul began to cry softly. The last time I'd seen him cry was at his mother's funeral more than 20 years ago. Because it was dark I could hear him more than I could see him. I knew his pain but I felt cold. The training I had gone through all these years was paying off: I had not only attended countless self-improvement seminars, I had also listened to numerous recorded programs on my favorite topic: self-mastery. I believed in the power of asking better questions, the importance of what we kept our focus on, the kind of language we used and the physiology we adopt. I had learned how to control my emotions and eliminate those which didn't serve me. Why was it so difficult to apply what I had learned?

I tried to focus on the good in this situation. I knew I should be asking myself questions such as: "What lessons will this situation teach me?" or "How will I help others with what I'm going through?"

But instead, the questions that were invading my thoughts were debilitating ones like: "How can this be happening to me?" or "How could he betray me in such a manner?" I simply had no energy to fight them.

I was comforted by the fact that Jean-Paul professed to still love me. I empathized because I knew how it felt to love two people simultaneously with the same degree of intensity. We had a strong relationship, though, and I was determined to save it.

"Without editing," I asked, "can you tell me how you feel right now?"

"I am relieved that I've told you."

"Good, what else do you feel?"

"I feel that I'm a very lucky man to be loved so selflessly. She doesn't expect anything at all."

Sure, that's what you think. I already decided that this girl had a hidden agenda. She is using the best tools she has—such as her helplessness, her chagrin and her past tragedies—to completely enthrall my husband. Didn't all men have a secret longing to be the rescuer, the knight in shining armor? He had obviously found one that needed extra care!

Who is this woman anyway? What did she do to make him fall in love with her? Even though he says she's not, I'm sure she is attractive. I've seen these Venezuelan beauties at every Miss Universe contest. They are stunning. He doesn't want me to worry, so he's downplaying it, but she must be gorgeous!

Then the friend and loving partner inside me found its voice:

"You know what darling, you deserve to be happy. You've given me a wonderful life all these years we've been together. I'll forever be grateful for that. I've not been the perfect wife and if you can find happiness elsewhere, I think you should go for it. You still have at least another half of your life to live. And to spend that second half with someone so much younger might be good for you."

I was saying all of this with my head. My heart had left the room ages ago. I felt such horrible, unbearable pain I could hardly control the emotion any longer. Jean-Paul squeezed my hand and stroked my head. It was probably hard for him to face the situation. I remembered my own dilemma of many years ago, battling with the feelings I had for Adam. And I also remembered how Jean-Paul had dealt with it. He had remained calm and convinced that everything would be all right.

'Be supportive and be understanding,' I encouraged myself silently. 'If he has any love left for you he'll be grateful.'

"So where do we go from here?" I asked, although I already knew the answer that would come back.

"I don't know."

Uncertainty, fear and panic were settling in. What disaster is striking me? What am I to do? This is my husband who has always loved me more than I've ever loved him. He is having an affair. He has fallen in love with another woman. My world is shattered. I want to cry. I want to die. What has happened to him? What tools was this woman using to entrap my husband?

I had to get out of this state of mind. At this point it was very late. Tomorrow would be another day and we'd figure out where to go from there.

I sought refuge in the bathroom, fearing that my insides might explode. The upset of the last few hours was taking its toll. How could I have imagined that this night was only a precursor to what was to befall us?

2

The reaction

On Saturday morning reality sank in. I cried my first tears, alone in the shower. I felt a great release. As my tears mixed with the water, I was being cleansed of some of the darkness of the past few days. The pain held on fast, though. I thought of the Korean woman who spoke at a conference I had attended in Dallas. She had told us about letting the tears go down the drain with the pain. I visualized the emotions I was fighting being washed away. I wanted to replace the fear, the hurt, the despair and the sense of betrayal by hope, peace, trust and compassion. I let the warm water run over my body for the longest time. I cried bitter tears, and cursed Jean-Paul, his secretary and the entire country she came from.

I dressed slowly, picked up a few of my journals from my bedside cabinet and found Jean-Paul in the kitchen fixing breakfast. I told him that I couldn't eat anything. I needed some time alone today. I reassured him that I'd be fine and that I'd be back later that evening.

I decided to seek refuge at a nearby bookstore. My plan was to pick up a book on how to fix a broken heart. That's how it felt. It was unbearable to think about facing life without my partner. He was my first love and my best friend. I was ready to fight with every ounce of energy I had left.

When I started the car, Ricky Martin's song "She's All I Ever Had" came on as the first track on the CD player. Jean-Paul had been the last person to drive my car. The line "She's my lover, she's my friend" hit me like a stab to the chest. Maybe it's their song, I thought. Maybe he thinks about Efelia when he hears that line. I don't remember anything about the

15-minute drive to the mall. I just couldn't get that song out of my head. I kept imagining them in bed kissing and loving one another. I couldn't stop the tears. I thought of confiding in Dana: she was my closest girl-friend, and she had experienced betrayal as well: her husband had actually left her to marry his secretary several years ago. She would understand my pain. I just couldn't find enough strength in me to speak to anyone about the situation. I would, in time, maybe when it was all over!

When I got to the bookstore, I found myself compelled to read my journals rather than pick up a book. I went back ten years.

March 19, 1990
Every day that goes by without a card or a call from Adam brings a new sadness and a bit of resignation. How could he care for me more than as a brother, a good friend? I've hallucinated that there was more because he's such a caring man. And when he held me in his arms and kissed me ever so lightly on the lips I surrendered in spirit to him.

March 20, 1990
A. called today and left a message. I told JP how delighted I was to have gotten a call. My husband is totally amazing and wonderful. My love for him is strengthened by his complete trust, his tolerance and understanding. He's just remarkable!

April 17, 1990
I missed Adam's call today. Wrote to him that I'd be on the next flight to Tampa if he just asked me to come.
Dana called tonight and we spoke for nearly an hour. She says to send the letter even though the part about being on the next flight to Tampa makes her nervous.

May 8, 1990
A. has invited me to come up to Toronto to a Sales Conference he is sched-uled to speak at. JP didn't object to my going; he was incredibly supportive and said that I was like a bird, and that he would leave the door of the

cage open so I could come back whenever I wished, and that if he closed the door and held me captive, I would probably die!

A. and I had lunch and dinner together. We danced a little, hugged a little, talked a lot and made no plans for the future.

May 10, 1990

JP surprised me with a dozen red roses when I returned home from Toronto. The card only said 'I love you!' It made me cry. I'm fortunate to be loved so much by my husband.

June 18, 1990

Saw A. today in Dallas, at the Conference. Seems like the magnetism he has over me will not lessen. As soon as I see him, my heart jumps in my chest.

He said he's stayed away from me to give me space and help me make a decision.

June 21, 1990

Adam and I hugged in the lobby of the Loews Hotel on our last day in Dallas, and I walked away, unable to hold back the tears. He says that he has very strong feelings for me. Do I not want to even give a try to a separation from JP and find out if I could be happy with A.?

July 8, 1990

Poor Jean-Paul is so patient and compassionate. He knows that right now, I am not in love with him. I could give up everything tomorrow if Adam asked me to marry him. The only thing that stops me is the pain I would cause JP and our daughters. One day my girls will leave me to have a life of their own and my husband might leave me for another woman. Then will I regret? Nothing is sacred in life. Nothing is forever. I am in turmoil.

◆   ◆   ◆

Reading through my old journals brought more tears. Jean-Paul always hated to see me cry. I needed to be brave and not let him see how desperate I felt. I wanted to fight to save our marriage with all my energy, and at the same time, I wanted him to believe that he was free to leave if that would make him happy. I remembered my friend Joelle's advice: "if your man ever confides in you that he is attracted to another woman, let him have his fun until he gets his fill. Otherwise, he might experience regret for a long time and resent you for having made him give up too soon what was a simple fling." Joelle was older than me, and I valued her opinion. I should maybe follow her advice.

I wanted to know more about men though. Why do they lie? Why do they have to carry on affairs even when they have a partner who never refuses herself to them? I also asked myself why happily married people often found themselves attracted to someone else. It was what we call in French *le fruit défendu* (the forbidden fruit).

I couldn't find answers to my many questions in the books I was picking up. I did choose one by Barbara De Angelis—*Secrets about Men Every Woman Should Know*. I spent most of the day reading, going through my old journals and writing in the new one.

I returned home at about 7 pm. On the way back I stopped off to buy a single yellow rose and a card. It said exactly what I wanted to express: 'I love you and I always will.' I added that I realized my life had been wonderful with him and that I really wanted to save our relationship. If he would have me, I wanted to be his for life.

Jean-Paul was outside watering our trees when I returned.

"Hi, how was your day?"

"Fine, I went to the bookstore. Yours?"

"Not so good. I felt abandoned."

"Oh well, *moi aussi!*" (me too!)

After dinner we went out for a walk. We held hands and talked. Jean-Paul reminded me that he loved me still. He said that he was in pain and he needed time to sort out his emotions.

When we got to bed, however, he distanced himself from me. I couldn't stand it and asked him to stop neglecting me. He touched my chest and stroked the heart area yet he didn't attempt to make love to me.

I started sobbing uncontrollably.

"Do you know that whenever a woman cries I always fear that it's because she is either hurt or afraid and I can't make love to her?"

I became hysterical. I had no sense of dignity left. Then he started to kiss me fiercely and made love to me with an eagerness bordering brusquerie.

◆   ◆   ◆

Every time I imagined my husband and his secretary together my heart ached and I wanted to scream. At times I wondered if what was happening was, in some bizarre way, God answering my prayers. Did my heart have to break so that it could grow to love again?

On Sunday evening Jean-Paul treated me to a loving session that reconnected us more closely than the previous night's.

"You know, darling, I will do whatever is necessary to save our relationship."

"Please don't fight me on that!" was his reply.

"I am going to fight with every ounce of energy so that our marriage survives this affair!"

This time, he remained silent.

◆   ◆   ◆

On Monday when Jean-Paul went back to the office, my emotions went absolutely wild. Danielle was in school, so I was home alone. An uncontrollable fury came over me without warning. As I emptied the dish-washer an overwhelming urge to break the glasses I was putting away hit me. One by one I hurled them onto the kitchen floor. I threw them with such anger and such force that they didn't just smash, they exploded into hundreds of thousands of pieces. An old Pyrex dish was next. I threw it so hard that it broke the tile it collided with. I felt totally possessed by a rage that needed an outlet. Had I owned a metal garbage can, I would have thrown in more stuff inside of it, since I had learned that the noise effect could be more therapeutic than the simple breaking of the dishes!

What triggered my outburst was that, for the first time in my life, I was jealous. Another woman had attracted my husband's affection. I had to know more about what had been going on. Were there letters? Were there presents? I ran into our bedroom and rummaged in his walk-in closet. On the floor I found an empty Perfumania bag. Had he bought her some per-fume? Madly I searched his closet, vainly sniffing everything. Still I hunted. Just as I was about to give up, well hidden in a corner where his shirts hung, under souvenir items from Maui, I found a 2-piece lady's bicycle outfit. The price tags were still attached: $49 a piece! I wanted to throw up. My Goodness! My husband, who never buys me clothing except for T-shirts from the overseas destinations his job took him to, had bought this woman the most expensive exercise outfit I had ever seen. I kept on searching and found other items too: shirts from Maui and from San Fran-cisco all in a lady's size small. I also discovered a Walkman CD player and two new CDs of two of my favorite artists, Ricky Martin and Yanni.

I curled up on the floor into the fetal position. I called to God for help and for strength. Don't let me hurt myself! Please help me change my focus and ask myself better questions than the ones that are like a broken record in my head: "How could this happen to us?", "How could he do this to me?"

After taking a long shower and crying some more, I put on my make-up and resolved to shake myself out of that debilitating state of mind. I needed to meditate. That was always one way to reconnect with what truly matters. The love in my heart. My faith. My inner peace. My oneness with my Creator. The meditation helped me to relax, although it took a very long time before I succeeded in shutting down the loud voices in my head. "Empty your mind, inhale deeply, exhale slowly, concentrate on the divine light. Concentrate on what you desire: Peace, Love, Joy, Forgiveness."

I considered myself fortunate that Jean-Paul had confided in me relatively early. I was thankful that I had a partner who trusted me enough to share with me his most intimate thoughts. I was lucky that he'd asked me for my help, my patience, my understanding and my forgiveness.

Our friends Barry and Sandra had briefly separated a couple of years before. Sandra had been suspecting his infidelity and she had set Barry up with a tape recorder in his car. It turned out that he had been fooling around with their secretary for the past five years! Sandra had beaten the living daylights out of him and broken her own wrist by punching him in the head in a fit of anger. She had also dragged the girl into the woods and hit her so hard she sent her to the hospital with her nose broken in three places! Sandra later confessed to me that if an off-duty policeman who heard loud screaming had not stopped her, she might have killed the girl! Sandra spent the night in jail and Barry had to post bail. Then he had to crawl, beg and kneel at her feet, asking for her forgiveness. Sandra seriously considered divorcing Barry. They had since reconciled and her outburst had probably kept Barry out of trouble.

I had told Sandra that if Jean-Paul ever betrayed me in this manner, I would just invite a couple of girlfriends to go on a cruise to the Greek Islands with me, use his credit cards and have my own fun there! Now that I was facing this real life situation, that option seemed totally unrealistic.

Was I playing the role of the tolerant and stoic wife, just like both his mother and mine had? I had never witnessed a heated argument between my parents. They never yelled at one another, and neither did his parents, not in front of us anyway. And I couldn't remember having ever seen my mother crying. Nevertheless, we both knew that our fathers had carried on affairs in our native Haiti, where it was quite common for married men to have a mistress. Jean-Paul and I very seldom raised our voices or used words that we might regret having said. This time had been no different. I had controlled my reaction in front of him. I would not let him see me overcome by emotion.

I couldn't help thinking about 'machismo' which remains a strong cultural influence in most Latin American countries. Although he had never shown himself as a chauvinist, I wondered if that was playing a part in Jean-Paul's need to seek the company of another woman. We both knew of several members of the Haitian society that were secretly admired because of their extramarital adventures. A story commonly told at my grandparents' dining table for example was that of a man we all knew who had become the lover of his wife's sister-in-law. His wife's brother had nearly caught him in the act. It was one of those big Haitian scandals, yet most people laughed and even admired Fernand for his exploits. He had actually led not just a double life, but a triple life, since he had also fathered two children with another woman. Fernand had become nothing short of a legend because of his adventures. On the other hand, the women who dared to have relations outside of marital vows were considered as *femmes de mauvaise vie* (women of little virtue) and often became outcasts of society.

After my mother passed away, my father criticized one of her married girlfriends who had taken a lover. I told him he had no right to badmouth anyone, considering he'd been with other women himself while married to my mother. I asked him how he would have felt if my mother had taken a lover, and why should it be only men that were entitled to extramarital affairs? He had remained speechless, too shocked to reply.

Was it a displaced pride that was forcing me to keep such a façade in my husband's presence and have my outbursts when all alone?

I comforted myself with thoughts of how Jean-Paul had always treated me during all our years together: wasn't it just a couple of years ago when he surprised me on our wedding anniversary? He had flown to Houston for work on the Tuesday after Memorial Day and our anniversary was on the Wednesday. Since he'd be back to Southlake for the weekend, I had told him we'd celebrate then, and asked him not to send me any flowers until Friday. Of course, being like most women I know, I could say something and mean the opposite. I still expected some flower arrangement on our special day. When I got home and didn't find any I was somewhat disappointed. I searched the entire house, thinking my daughters might have hidden the flowers somewhere. I looked inside their closets, and ours. Nothing! A blinking light on our answering machine alerted me that someone had called. The message was from a local florist who reassured me that an attempt to deliver flowers had been made but they had the wrong address. I was thrilled when a beautiful arrangement of two dozens of multi colored long-stem roses was brought to my home by the store-owner herself. I called Jean-Paul a couple of times to thank him but I kept getting his answering machine.

I was just getting out of the shower when he finally called back. We had a phone line in our spacious bathroom and I took the call right there, while air-drying in my newborn suit. I expressed my surprise and delight for the flowers. As I hung up the phone and looked in my bathroom mirror, I saw the reflection of a man standing behind me. It was Jean-Paul! He had flown back to Dallas that evening; rented a car and come in through the garage into our kitchen. He was hiding inside the pantry when he called me, and he had walked into our bedroom suite right after hanging up the phone to surprise me! He had also invited me to pack an overnight bag because he was taking me to my favorite restaurant and then to a hotel for the night.

I remember my initial reaction. When I first saw his reflection, I held on to my chest laughing and crying at the same time. I fell to the floor in a state of complete shock. He was laughing as well and we were on the tiled floor for several minutes enjoying ourselves like two kids. One aspect of our relationship I really cherish is the great fun we have together.

I resolved to continue working on rekindling the relationship. I knew that if I wanted to overcome this hurdle I would have to become more loving and more appreciative, and that I should also take better care of myself.

If this woman who now shared his bed had asked him for an exercise outfit, she must be into physical fitness. And that probably meant flat abs, tight buns, and an overall toned body, which was more than what I could show for myself. Maybe this was the incentive I needed to start working out.

My excuse had always been that I weighed the same 116 lbs as on my wedding night, give or take a pound or two. This was normal for my 5 foot 3 frame, and I was in excellent physical shape, enjoying a pretty high level of energy. My body could certainly use some toning and if that Efelia girl cycled like a pro, then I needed to bring my old bike out and start exercising to get in better form.

◆　　　◆　　　◆

When Jean-Paul arrived home from work that evening I had completely regained my senses. He would never guess what fury was unleashed earlier. I had cleaned up my mess. I did not bring up the fact that I had found his gifts for his secretary and how painful that had been. The millions of pieces of glass had been swept away, the gifts for his secretary back in their corner under his shirts.

We slept in each other's arms. He knew that I was hurting and said he was sorry.

The following evening we had dinner at the home of our dearest friends Travis and Yvette. Jean-Paul was his usual old self. Was he pretending for my sake that everything was wonderful in our world?

He was charming and loving, proudly looking at me and teasing me in front of our friends. They never suspected that anything was different in our lives.

Julio Iglesias' song *"La Carretera"* was playing in their living room and Jean-Paul asked me if I wanted to dance. I would have loved to be in my husband's arms but I was on my guard. I couldn't let him hurt me anymore than he already had. He was set to leave the following day for Caracas and my heart bled every time I imagined his reunion with his secretary. He said that he wished he could promise me that they would just talk when they got together but it would be misleading me. And I knew it too.

3

*The confusion
(Jean-Paul)*

None of the tropical beauties Venezuela is known for had caught my interest until I met Efelia. When one has the best the rest do not matter and Mia had been my only love for more than thirty years. We had been separated for long periods of time over the past several years. Mia often said that these separations had probably saved our marriage because they gave us breathing space. When we reconnected it often felt like a honeymoon.

My company sent me away for several days at a time, and sometimes for several weeks or months. It all depended on the project I was involved in. Venezuela had been the latest in a series of overseas assignments. Mia and I had gotten used to being apart.

How did I let myself fall in love with Efelia? First she started confiding in me about her tragedies. And I wanted to offer her moral support. Then the romantic guy in me wondered how I could help her get over her pain. That is when I started thinking that we were soul mates. When she declared her love for me I was flattered and also quite happy. She seemed sincere and genuine.

When I found out about my own feelings for her it was too late and nothing could stop the flow of tenderness that was drawing me towards her. I wanted to give her a desire to live, a desire to achieve her dreams. Without realizing it, I started to include myself in those dreams. I had told Efelia how much I loved my wife and family from the very first time we spoke. So, I don't think she expected much from me except a short-lived romance, but it was intense. She called what we had *un regalo de Dios*—a gift from God.

We actually met the very first time I visited Venezuela. As the Project Assistant, she had been assigned to take care of the needs of the entire group that was working on my company's Caracas project. She was very attentive to the needs of all the expatriates that were part of the project, showing great dedication in making our stay in Venezuela as pleasant as possible. She took great pride in her country and wanted to help us discover its beauty.

One rainy night, the company vehicle didn't show up to pick me up. Efelia remained in the office with me for over two hours, to make sure that a company driver would come and take me back to my hotel. She seemed more concerned about my safety than about her own. While waiting for the car to arrive, she confided in me about her tragic life. Her father's suicide five years ago had deeply affected her. She thought of ending her own life when she found herself pregnant and the baby's father decided to marry someone else. Only the love she had for her son kept her alive.

Efelia broke my heart with all her sad stories. Her first big love when she was 25-years old had asked her in marriage. One week after proposing, he had died of a heart attack. Her parents had divorced when she was very young and she had not been able to visit her father as often as she wanted. Her relationship with her mother was strained.

I've always been a good listener. She needed someone to talk to. We soon became friends. One Saturday, when I asked her to help me find a driver and a car to visit the city, she showed up with her three-year old son in the chauffeured car and took me to City Hall and the historical part of town.

I invited her to lunch a few times, then we had dinner together. On weekends we went dancing on a few occasions and one night as I held her in an embrace, I realized that I wanted more than her friendship.

Efelia writes very well. Her letters helped me discover her kind heart. She had suffered a great deal and I wanted to protect her from further hurt in life. I wanted to be like an older brother for her since she was an only child.

The first time I accompanied her to her home, I was quite surprised to discover the neighborhood in which she lived. The taxi dropped us off at the bottom of 40 long steps, leading to narrow alleys only walkers could use. The homes were very modest and very close together. This was an area of Caracas that I knew existed but was seeing for the first time. Efelia was obviously embarrassed to take me there and it was only when I insisted, that she let me walk her all the way to her front door. She lived with her mother, her son, and the mother's common-law husband, who was the boy's godfather. She told me that she had not had a boyfriend since her son's birth.

Efelia always took great interest in my senseless conversations. She was intelligent and a teaser by nature. She always showed a sensitive side but remained in control of her emotions. Sometimes, the sadness in her eyes revealed her mood and that almost broke my heart.

I wondered how I could ever tell Mia about my feelings for my secretary.

I was eighteen and Mia was barely fourteen years old when we first met. Mia told me that her heart skipped a beat when I came in to purchase an album at *La Boite à Musique*, (the Music Box), her uncle's record store where she was working during the Christmas holiday. She reminded me many times over the years that right then and there she knew that I was the man she'd eventually marry. It really was love at first sight for both of us, because I had noticed her as well. Two months later I asked her to become my girlfriend.

We have been together all these years. When I left Haiti to study at the University of Puerto Rico, Mia obtained a scholarship and went to Spain to study at the University of Madrid. The five years that we spent away from one another added muscles to our relationship and when we met on holidays we enjoyed our time together. We have kept hundreds of letters that we exchanged during our separation, in which we spoke of our undying love and made plans for the day when we would marry. Right after I graduated from college we went back to Haiti for our traditional wedding with family and friends, before moving to New York City where Mia had already found us a place to live.

When our first born was 10 months old, Mia quit her job at the United Nations to accompany me to Tokyo, the first of many overseas assignments my job would require. We spent a year in Japan. I hoped that the company would send us as a family for many more assignments overseas. It unfortunately was not to be. For several years I traveled alone for extended periods of time. At times I felt that I had failed in my role as father: our girls were growing up without my constant presence in their lives. I know the family suffered because of the time I spent away from home. Now that our daughters were older, my absences were for longer periods of time. When I came home, they often asked me why I thought I could interfere in their lives when I was there only for short visits. I was spending more time away rather than at home.

And now, for the first time in the history of our marriage, I had come home to Mia with news that risked shaking the foundation of our marriage. The way I felt toward Efelia made me wonder if that was the way Mia felt toward her Adam and I understood better the dilemma she experienced several years ago. I remembered my feeling of helplessness and the uncertainty when my wife had confided in me how she felt towards her millionaire friend.

I wondered if she was just infatuated with him and I assured her that I would survive even if she left me for him. I don't know for sure that she ever considered that eventuality, but I chose to let her go to him without showing either anger or resentment. It took a lot of self-control, and all the emotional balance I had not yet mastered to remain calm under the circumstances.

Her Adam was not only handsome—in her eyes—and intelligent, he was very successful financially, an entrepreneur who had made millions in his ventures. I remember Mia's reaction every time he called. She would not even try to hide her excitement. He became her spiritual mentor. They exchanged a few letters, several phone calls, met at different conventions the network marketing company they both worked for sponsored. One day she told me that she was in love with him.

When I met him at one of their national events in Phoenix, I did feel a twinge of envy. That wealthy man was not only in great physical shape, he was also a sharp dresser, played the guitar and wrote poetry, and all that always attracted my wife's attention.

He motivated Mia to develop her sales organization, teaching her the principles he had used to become a top producer. He introduced her to Brian Tracy's *Psychology of Achievement,* a program that influenced both our lives as well as that of our children. It was also thanks to him that Mia discovered her love of public speaking. Her mentor encouraged her to become a trainer for their company. Despite her French accent, she was chosen to speak in front of 2000 people when the company's president visited New Jersey. She loved the limelight and when I accompanied her to some of the functions held in major cities of the US or Canada, I often introduced myself as Mr. Mia!

I wasn't sure how I would have reacted if they had become lovers. I only knew that I had readied myself for that possibility. Whenever they met at their sales conferences, I wondered if that would be the occasion when the affair took on another dimension. It never did.

I once said to Mia after her infatuation for her Adam had vanished:

"Your friend does not know what he missed out on. If he had ever made love to you, he might have never let you go!"

"Why do you say that?" she asked.

"Because you're the most passionate and the best lover I've ever had. I'm a very lucky man!"

◆　　　◆　　　◆

Mia was not only my first love. She was my forever friend. She was my life's companion. She broke my heart when we said goodbye at the Dallas Fort Worth Airport when I flew out to be back here in Caracas. Mia's acceptance of the circumstances was at the same time comforting and tormenting. She was hiding her tears behind dark sunglasses. She asked me to let her know everything and to not worry too much about hurting her feelings.

I thanked her for her trust. I knew how difficult it must be for her and I appreciated her letting me go. It showed how much she loved me.

In an e-mail I sent that same afternoon I promised to be very truthful with her:

> *I will let you know what I am thinking and what I am doing. I'm sure it was hard for you when I described the intensity of my affection for E. I didn't do it to break your heart. You're not responsible for my straying. I had decided to start working on bettering our relationship and on defining our common goals. What has happened was totally unexpected.*

I was in such torment while in Venezuela. I hated myself for causing my wife so much pain. I threw myself alone into that abyss and it was for me alone to find the rope to get myself out of it. I did not wish to hurt anyone. But love causes pain and can tear hearts apart. I was sorry that I couldn't hide my affection for someone else. Now that everything was out in the open, I had to face the facts but I too felt hurt. How could I enjoy myself when I knew that I was responsible for so much pain?

A few days into the Caracas trip, I received a letter from Mia. It comforted me to know that she was being brave in spite of all the challenges. I was depressed. I'd be breaking Mia's heart if I stayed with Efelia. And leaving Efelia now would surely break her own heart. I felt torn. In the letter, Mia was suggesting that we separate and I told her that it shouldn't be necessary. I asked her to give me a little time to sort out my feelings.

I tried to find flaws in Efelia, in the hope that it would help me to forget her but found nothing significant. I thought that I would perhaps be her lover for a short time but would remain her friend for life. Knowing how much pain Mia was going through made me feel awful.

In my e-mail back I asked the friend I had in my wife to be patient with this sentimental husband of hers:

> *Could you still have faith in me for a while longer? Give me time to repair my tormented heart and to see the future more clearly. Please do not hold a grudge. Forgive me for all the pain I am causing you.*

How could I have suspected that the present pain was nothing compared to what we would soon be facing? How could I have imagined what was in store for us and how the relationship was going to be shaken at its core?

4

The decision

We next met in Hawaii. I flew out there first, with Jean-Paul due to arrive a few days later. We were both participating in a seminar at the Waikoloa Hilton on the Big Island of Hawaii.

This resort is one of the most exquisite in the world and I never missed the opportunity to return when asked to volunteer my services to staff a yearly self-improvement seminar. The event brought participants from all over the world, and Jean-Paul had decided to attend it this time. Since the focus was on mastering both the physical and emotional aspects of one's life, I had encouraged him to sign up as an attendee. I was now hoping that the segment by a relationship expert might help us both in our current situation.

The grounds of the Waikoloa resort are magnificent. The walk from the vast open-air lobby to the adjacent towers leads you through a covered hallway where stunning pieces of Asian art are displayed. It is a very exclusive open-air museum. Guests can hop on either a boat or a train to be transported from one tower to the next or from the pool area to any of the several restaurants the resort offers.

I was staying with most of the crew at a villa across the street from the Hilton. It was a pleasant 10-minute walk thanks to the lush landscaping and breathtaking ocean views. I felt reenergized as soon as I stepped barefoot on the grass next to one of the spectacular pools of the Waikoloa.

The first night, I called Jean-Paul. I couldn't help noticing how cold and distant he was on the telephone. It was as if he didn't want to talk to me or be with me. He had just returned from Caracas and would spend a couple of days with our daughters before joining me in Kona. He was clearly still in his other world. Maybe I no longer belonged to his world. I felt neglected, unwanted and unloved. French poet Lamartine's words echoed in my head : « *Un seul être vous manque et tout est dépeuplé.* » (If only one person is absent the universe seems deserted.)

I felt utterly alone.

The next day started off in a magical way, though. As I walked into the hotel reception area, I caught sight of a dear friend, Dylan. I thought of him as my lover boy. He was from Australia, 33 years old, tall and athletic. We had met earlier in the year in Maui while we were both attending another seminar.

Dylan wore a tight sleeveless black shirt which showed off his chiseled torso. He wasn't overly muscular, just toned. He had a dazzling smile and wore his black hair in a neatly-trimmed style, in contrast to the ponytail he had the last time I had seen him. He seemed to have lost quite a bit of weight and in summary looked dashing.

Without saying a word, Dylan held me in an embrace that gave me an enormous boost at a moment when I desperately needed to feel loved and adored. I looked into his deep blue eyes and totally immersed myself in this bath of pure, unconditional, non-sexual love. We'd had a great connection back in January and had exchanged a few letters and phone calls in the meantime. He surprised me with his tight hug and light kisses on my neck.

"Hey gorgeous! How have you been?"

"Oh my, Dylan! What a surprise. You look fabulous! How much weight have you lost?"

"Thirty pounds."

"Wow! Amazing. It is so good to see you again. How is life treating you?"

"I can't complain. How about you? How is everything?"

"I'm glad you're here. I could use a good shoulder to lean on. Maybe we can have a drink tonight?"

"What's going on? You're sure you don't want to talk about it?"

"I really can't right now but if you'd like we can get together later."

"Sure, call me after dinner."

◆   ◆   ◆

I spent the day deep in thought. I busied myself with my crew duties and welcomed the distraction the registering participants created. I had to face up to reality. Jean-Paul would not be in a position to offer me the love I'd been craving for some time. At least not until he got over his feelings for Efelia, that is. What would I do in the meantime? I would continue to love him and show patience and understanding.

After dinner, Dylan and I spent a couple of hours under the stars on a hammock near the Dolphin pool of the Waikoloa. We were between the ocean and the Laguna listening to the soothing sound of the waves and enjoying a perfect night. He listened to me empty my soul of all the heartache of the past few weeks.

I confided in Dylan that I did not know how I was supposed to act toward my husband at a time when he did not want to be with me with the same intensity as in the past. I wanted to remain distant so that he'd feel that I was letting go of him. At the same time I craved his touch and his love. I allowed myself to be cuddled by Dylan and justified this weakness as my way of assuring that I would not appear too eager for Jean-Paul's affection when I saw him the next day. Dylan was extremely proper and I thanked him for having been such a comforting listener when he walked me back to my condo across the street from the Waikoloa resort. He just hugged me and kissed me on the cheek. I felt loved and cherished by my young Aussie friend.

◆   ◆   ◆

When I picked him up at the airport in a convertible Mustang I'd borrowed from my buddy Annie, I was wearing flowers in my hair. As I put a lei around his neck, my husband looked at me as if he were seeing me with new eyes. He told me that I had a beautiful smile. I remained cool. He was showing affection but nothing more.

When we retired to our condo he made himself busy on his computer. I wanted him to make love to me but, I guess, he wanted to keep the memory of his last encounter with his secretary alive.

At that moment I wished I were with Dylan. Or was it Jean-Paul that I desired but since he showed no interest in me I longed to be with my Aussie friend? I was confused.

I wanted to be held and comforted. I felt neglected by my husband. He was aloof. He asked if he could show me pictures of Efelia and I acquiesced. It was an unusual request, yet I understood him wanting me to see what she looked like. In one taken of the two of them together, he looked happy and somewhat younger. She looked very young and somewhat unpretentious: from what I could see, she wore little make up. I tried to find in her what might have attracted him to her. He had been truthful when he told me she was not a great beauty. Yet I felt a twinge of something. Maybe it was jealousy. Maybe it was the age factor. Jean-Paul was 52, I was 48. She was in her mid thirties. There was also the uncertainty, the fear that my husband might have really fallen in love with this girl. Maybe he wanted me to allow him to continue seeing her while working in Venezuela.

I prayed a silent prayer: "Dear God, please bring him back to his senses. I cannot tolerate another woman in our lives. I can't stand the very thought of it. Please make him realize that what we have is unique. Our love has lasted decades. This girl can't just seduce my husband and destroy our marriage!"

I was thinking of so many of our friends who had gotten divorced because of infidelity. I remembered the suffering some families had gone through. Fernand's wife for example, the man with the two mistresses, had been unable to forgive him, even after his death from a heart attack. She had told their children about their father's lifestyle, and had been angry most of her remaining years. She had developed a cancer which might have been triggered by Fernand's scandalous behavior. The children did acknowledge their half-siblings as they grew up. But that only happened after Fernand's wife had joined him in the thereafter.

◆   ◆   ◆

Jean-Paul suggested we go out to dinner on our third night in Hawaii. At the end of our meal he took my hand in his: "Darling, I want you to know what I have decided. I'm going to end the relationship with Efelia as soon as I return to Caracas."

This was happening earlier than I had expected. The seminar had not even covered Relationship Mastery and he had already come to a decision! I didn't know how to react to this piece of news and I couldn't help but be slightly skeptical:

"I'm sure you'll understand if I abstain from making any comment."

"I can't bear to see you go through this torment," he replied. "I've decided, and she already suspects that it will come to this. It will be better this way. I don't like to see you so sad and so thin."

I had not realized how much the few pounds I had lost in the past weeks were showing: Jean-Paul had undoubtedly noticed the change as well. Also, I wasn't my usual exuberant self and many of my friends had asked me what was troubling me. I simply had lost my sparkle. What my husband was suggesting was good news indeed but I couldn't rejoice just yet. I still needed to see whether or not he'd keep his word.

◆　　◆　　◆

We kept each other at arm's length for the rest of the week and we spent our last day in Kona lounging near one of the pools of the hotel, next to a cascading waterfall. Coincidentally, Dylan was on the sun bed next to mine. He looked great with his nicely tanned and toned body in his tight swim trunks. I was happy to be sitting close to him. Girls much younger than me were eying him and probably envying the attention I was getting from him. One girl in particular who had been his partner during the seminar had wanted to get closer to him, and was now trying to speak to him. He dismissed her by offering to apply suntan lotion on my back. I let him rub me from my neck to my toes. Jean-Paul was with his friends from the seminar and I was flirting shamelessly with my lover boy.

When it was time for lunch, Dylan said he would have to leave soon. He sat on my lounge chair. Our eyes locked into an intense look. He was so handsome I wanted to kiss him.

"Thank you so much for everything! Thanks for the hugs when I needed them, and for being such a good listener when I was pouring my heart out. You were so good to me."

Before I realized what was happening, Dylan's lips were on mine. He took my breath away and satisfied my secret desire.

"Oh dear, what a yummy kiss that was! What was that for?" I blurted out, while catching my breath.

"That's so you know how desirable you are!"

At that very moment Jean-Paul returned with a snack he had purchased at the nearby poolside cafe. He had seen us and spoke to me in French, possibly so that Dylan wouldn't understand.

"*Tu pourrais être plus discrète.*" (You could be more discreet)

"*C'était spontané et une surprise pour moi!*" (It was spontaneous and a surprise for me) I replied.

Jean-Paul ate his snack while feeling slightly ignored. Both men obviously had self esteem high enough to allow them to handle this awkward situation with ease.

When it was time for Dylan to leave, I wanted to be kissed again, and this time I didn't care how Jean-Paul would react. I got up and told him I'd be right back. Without a glance in his direction, I left my towel, my beach bag and my magazine on the sun bed, draped myself in my Hawaiian wrap and told Dylan I'd walk him to his room. In a way I was getting back at Jean-Paul, giving him a taste of his own medicine.

As soon as the door of his hotel room closed behind us, Dylan was kissing me and squeezing me in his arms. I let myself go and thoroughly enjoyed his demonstration. I could sense his ardor and I let him play with me for a short while. He gave me one last hug, one last kiss, promised to call me from Sidney and asked me to let him know how things turned out between Jean-Paul and me.

When I returned to the poolside, Jean-Paul gave me an inquisitive look: "Should I be concerned?" he asked.

"Not unless I decide to fly to Australia next week." I replied. I knew he was puzzled. I knew he wanted to ask me exactly what was happening between Dylan and me. I considered that Jean Paul and I were going through a separation of sorts. He had strayed. That was reason enough for me to want to separate. We were still sleeping in the same bed, but he had shared his with another woman and I felt entitled to my freedom. I didn't think I owed my unfaithful husband any explanation about my behavior. Besides what were hugs and kisses compared to what was going on between him and his secretary? I knew he'd said he would put a stop to the relationship. How could I know for sure that he would?

◆   ◆   ◆

When we got back to the reality of our Southlake surroundings, life seemed to be on hold. I knew in my heart that my husband was still in love with another woman and that he was still attracted and attached to her.

A woman's intuition does not normally fail her. When we made love I wondered if he fantasized about her. I didn't want to get hurt again. I held back. I did not surrender entirely. I kept saying to myself that I needed to keep part of my heart to myself so I would not hurt too much.

Soon it was time for Jean-Paul to return to Venezuela and he repeatedly assured me that there would no longer be any physical intimacy between him and Efelia. I did want to believe him but I could only pray that he'd keep his promise.

Jean-Paul was usually a man of his word. One of the aspects of our relationship that I've always treasured is how we can confide entirely in one another and trust that we will both show understanding and forgiveness. One of my not-so-happily married friends had declared that all men eventually cheat on their wives. We had been married for about ten years when she made this comment and I attempted to defend some of the husbands I knew, including my own. My friend said I should ask Jean-Paul about it and watch his reaction carefully.

When I asked him what he thought of the idea that most men needed to be with other women, he had simply replied: "It depends on the man." I hadn't been completely satisfied by the answer. I had made him promise that he would tell me if he ever strayed.

I was thankful that if he had some encounters with other women, it was in faraway lands. It never occurred to me to threaten to leave him if he ever strayed. In retrospect, I probably showed too much tolerance. He already knew that I would forgive.

What Jean-Paul and I had between us was sacred. I thought of it as the melting of two souls that are eternally connected. I knew I could trust him to confide in me if he ever got involved with someone else.

Jean-Paul had also wanted to be reassured that if I ever had a fling, it wouldn't be with someone he knew, and least of all with a man from our native land. I had told him he had nothing to worry about. He was my lover, my one and only love.

To have Jean-Paul as my best friend as well was priceless. I could confide in him if I felt attracted to other men, as had been the case with Adam and Dylan. And he knew that he could trust me with his confidences. I was not a jealous wife. I was assured of his deep love for me, and I never feared that he might leave me for anyone. It was unthinkable that he could have fallen in love with someone else. What if his infatuation was longer lasting than just these few months?

I thanked Jean-Paul for his decision to be just friends with Efelia. My heart needed time to heal. I was full of uncertainties, doubts and hallucinations that they were still carrying on a deep, intimate relationship even if there was no sex involved. I feared that they were hiding some secret from me. I felt like the outsider.

Jean-Paul seldom shared with me the e-mails they exchanged. Was I not entitled to know what took place between them? I was consumed with jealousy, and it was mixed with a silent rage. I was fearful and apprehensive. The carefree and self-assured woman I used to be was not around at the moment.

I decided to exercise patience. I told Jean-Paul that I admired his strength of character and his decision to sacrifice his pleasurable idyll so that I could stop crying and being miserable. I wondered if he was ready to sever the ties or if he just did it because he had said he would do it.

I was baffled when he admitted to me that he was more concerned about how Efelia would react to the breakup than how I would have reacted if he'd left me! He pointed out that he knew I had the necessary tools to help me cope in the face of any situation. She did not. Therefore, he wanted to spare her! I also realized that she had told him that she had wanted to kill herself when she had suffered a great sorrow. Maybe he now feared that she might do something stupid when he broke up with her. That was one sure way of manipulating someone to stay with you!

I wanted to scream! How could a woman he barely knew take over his life to the point where he gave her feelings priority over mine? Hadn't we been together more than 30 years? Did it not matter? I kept wondering what kind of hold that girl had on him. Could it be something we couldn't fight? This line of thinking on my part was helping me cope with the unthinkable. The unthinkable? He loved someone else more than he loved me! Someone he admitted himself was "not that pretty". What could make him feel the way he did toward her?

5

The complication (Jean-Paul)

When I returned to Venezuela in early October I didn't get a chance to tell Efelia that I had decided she and I should be just friends. She called me first to say that she was preoccupied. She had missed a period. I pleaded with her that she had to be mistaken. This was impossible. Not so impossible after all: I remembered that we had been careless on a couple of occasions.

This could not happen to me. This was the type of thing that happened to other people. I asked her to go and have the test done.

When she telephoned with the results and said that her suspicions had been confirmed, I lashed out. I was in the field, using a friend's cellular telephone and I went outside the building, gasping for air!

"This is crazy!" I screamed. "How can you let something like this happen? Don't you know my wife might leave me when she finds out?"

She started crying and her obvious distress would break anyone's heart. But, on this occasion, mine was as cold as steel. I remembered that she had told me how difficult it had been for her to conceive her first child. Had she lied to me? Selfishly I was shifting the blame to Efelia, but deep inside I knew that I was as much to blame since I should have been more careful.

That was the last thing I needed! Not now that I had just promised my wife that everything was over between Efelia and me. Not after I had decided that the relationship would no longer be intimate. How could Mia ever forgive me if I now told her that Efelia was pregnant?

All the promises I had made to my wife and to myself were worthless. What would I say to my forgiving partner? Could she ever show understanding and tolerance for something of this magnitude?

In one of our discussions, Efelia and I had discussed abortion, and we were both against it. Efelia hinted that she would do anything that I would ask her to do. I then asked if she would want to have an abortion. She refused to consider the alternative, then childishly and proudly suggested that she and her unborn baby could vanish from my life forever. We both knew right then that what she was suggesting was out of the question. I'm not sure she realized what kind of impact her condition would have on my relationship with Mia. In my anguished state, I kept wondering how she might have wanted for this to happen. I had heard stories about women from her country. They would do anything to get pregnant with a foreigner in order to obtain financial support for themselves and their baby. Although I knew deep in my heart that Efelia was not like that, in these circumstances I was willing to think anything to avoid claiming responsibility for this situation.

For the next couple of hours, I walked aimlessly around the complex, in the jungle of Morichal. It was the closest I'd ever been to hysterics. What was going to happen to my marriage? What had I done? How could I break this news to Mia? How would she react? I couldn't tell her on the telephone. I would have to do it in person, put her in a better mindset first, just like I had learned at a mastery seminar. I would first help bring her spirits very high, then I would deliver this devastating news to her. The contrast between pleasure and pain should diminish the impact.

And how should I treat Efelia? I had to tell her of my decision to stop being intimate with her. It wasn't going to be easy, in her state. She will think that it was because of the pregnancy. And then poor Mia had been so pleased with my decision to not allow the relationship with Efelia to continue. She could not imagine what calamity was striking us. This new development was the worse thing that could happen to us.

From the beginning, I had never led Efelia to believe that she could expect anything from me except a short-lived romance. This getting pregnant was not something I had ever considered could happen between us. Of course, I had allowed the romantic in me to fantasize about having two wives, in two different parts of the world, two women that were very different from each other.

The last time we had met, Efelia's inquisitive and sometimes sad look touched me deeply. I wanted to help her so much. She was shy and vulnerable, and had endeared herself to my heart with the gentle way she had with words.

I had been giving her self-help books and had shared with her what she needed to become the powerful woman she could be. She had complained that it was difficult for her to read entire books in English. I had found a Spanish version of Stephen Covey's *7 Habits of Highly Effective People,* and also John Gray's *How to Get What You Want and Want What You Have,* that she was reading. I was hoping that these books would help her in her circumstances.

When she came to my hotel to say goodbye, right before I was returning home to Texas, I told her of my decision to end our relationship. Efelia said that she always knew that her dream would end someday. She nevertheless felt the pain of the break up and so did I. And because of her condition, it was harder to find herself alone at this time.

We talked, hugged and reassured one another that the friendship would remain even if the romance was ending.

She was sad but didn't cry. The feelings we had for one another would help us survive this trial, knowing that we would always be there for each other. The sex had come as a small comfort for a tormented life. She had survived worse trials over the years than this heartache. What I wanted to give her was a new direction in life and the capacity to make decisions for a better future.

I knew it wouldn't be easy for me to forget my friend. I would still hold her close to my heart and her stoicism in front of this new trial made me appreciate her even more.

◆   ◆   ◆

I felt grateful to Mia for having been understanding about my involvement with my secretary. A few weeks earlier, in answer to an e-mail I'd sent, my wife had told me that she felt very lucky to be loved by me. She also had asked if I still wanted her as my spouse. Today, it was I who didn't know whether or not she'd still want me as her husband.

In her e-mail Mia had reminded me that she was my lifetime companion, my best friend and my partner. Would she still feel the same way when she found out that Efelia was pregnant?

In one of her more recent e-mails she wrote:

I love you forever. In just a week we will be together and I rejoice in antic- ipation of the love sessions we will indulge in. I am readying the massage oil, the candles, the bubbly bath and the champagne to celebrate our new relationship.

How ironic! Life was so unpredictable, especially when fate and circum- stances played tricks on us.

Sometimes I could put on a good act. One of the statements I often use is: "It's all small stuff." It helped me cope with reality. When I put things into perspective I convinced myself that the situation could have been much worse. I still had my health, my family and a good income. My problems were indeed 'small stuff' even if they appeared overwhelming and devastating. There were always millions of people who would love to have our lifestyle and cope with our problems rather than their own.

I asked Mia to make a reservation at a hotel for the Saturday night after I returned home. I told her that I needed to do some soul-searching and wanted to be alone with her away from the world.

I could only pray that she would be forgiving and that this new development would not destroy our marriage. I had so much at stake. Would our lives be shattered because of my carelessness? I couldn't stop asking myself how I could have allowed something of this magnitude to happen to me!

6

The explosion

It was the end of October when Jean-Paul returned home to Southlake. I picked him up at the airport and greeted him with my most radiant smile. My heart was smiling, it was light, and I was once again the happiest woman in the world. I had faith in our future. Jean-Paul had stopped his involvement with his secretary and life was beautiful again. I was in love and I was loved!

On Saturday night, as he had requested, we checked into the Marriott Hotel in Solana, 15 minutes away from our home. We had a lovely dinner at the hotel's restaurant and back in our hotel room Jean-Paul treated me to a slow, sensuous massage followed by a love session that brought me to ecstasy, a climax not experienced in quite some time. He held me for a very long while in his arms afterwards and asked me the most puzzling question.

"What would it take for you to leave me?"

I hesitated a few moments.

"Darling, if I didn't leave you when you admitted falling in love and having an intimate relationship with your secretary, I don't think anything could make me leave you."

I paused for a few seconds.

"Well … if you ever beat me up or if you gave me some deadly disease I would leave you!"

Then more seriously:

"Why are you asking?"

He put the question to me again:

"Is there anything else that would make you leave me?"

This time I asked him if there was something he wanted to tell me.

"Are you still seeing her? Did you break up with her or not? Are you still in love with her?"

His replies should have appeased me. Yet I sensed there was something he wasn't saying. He kept sighing and shaking his head.

"Can you guess what I have to say?"

So there was indeed something important that he couldn't bring himself to say outright. What could that be? Had Efelia given him some disease? He wouldn't have made love to me like he just had if it had been the case though. Had he met someone else? That was highly unlikely. Was he gay? No way. So, what then could it be? Then it dawned on me ...

"She's not pregnant, is she?"

The look on his face said it all. Fear as to how I would react, guilt and shame were all etched into his expression. I saw it in a flash but I needed to hear him confess.

"So is she pregnant then?" I asked more forcefully.

He nodded and in a barely audible voice:

"I am sorry."

My thoughts were racing. Why couldn't he just come right out and tell me? Why make me guess? What a fool I'd been to dream that it was all going to be so wonderful from now on. This cannot be happening! I may as well be dead. How could I survive such shame? I am going out of my mind! That cannot be true. How could something like this happen now? And why doesn't the woman just get an abortion? Why does she have to keep this baby? She just wants to wreck our marriage. That's all! I'm going to need to see proof that it's even my husband's baby. Didn't he say she has a son already? Then she knows exactly what she's doing. She's going to make sure she gets financial support from my husband. What a f ... whore! They must have done it on purpose so they could remain forever attached to one another. I remembered him saying that she would always be his friend. Well she had made sure that her attachment to my husband was now going to be everlasting.

What an insult to me. What a slap in the face. There was now going to be a constant reminder of their liaison in the child that she was going to give him. And what if that child was a boy? He couldn't give me a boy and now he might have one with this girl! I felt sick to my stomach. I was full of bitterness and felt such excruciating pain in my heart that I feared it might explode. Does intense emotional pain ever cause a heart attack? If so, then I might be having one. I wanted to run into another room. I wanted to scream! But I was in a hotel room. I was stuck here. I had nowhere else to go. I wanted to be in my own bed, in my own room, in my own home. Why did he bring me here to break this devastating news to me? Was it maybe to prevent the memory I'd have of this awful moment from being triggered every time I entered the sanctuary of our bedroom?

I felt numb. I chose numbness and indifference over anger, rage and despair which were all fighting to take the lead in my emotions. I was hyperventilating. I was suffocating with a mixture of disgust, shame, grief, despair. I wanted to wake up from the worst nightmare of my life. Except I was fully awake and Jean-Paul was saying something to me:

"Can I read something I wrote in my journal for you?"

I barely shrugged my shoulders, and quietly stayed in my corner of the bed, too shocked to speak, with thoughts that my world had just been shattered again, and this time in a worse fashion than ever before. Jean-Paul shared for several long moments, words written to describe his state of mind.

I didn't utter a single word. I didn't comment on the tears I saw on his face. I didn't comment on the things he had written. I wanted to sleep and wake up in another room, in another world. This couldn't be happening to us. Not now that the relationship was mending. Not now that I had let myself fall in love with him all over again. Not now that I had become so hopeful for our future together.

When he stopped reading I got up without a word. I could feel the blood pumping inside my head, as if it were about to explode, I felt sick to my stomach, sick to my heart. I locked myself in the bathroom and took the longest and hottest shower I'd ever taken. I allowed the tears to flow freely. I didn't scream. I just sobbed and banged my head on the bathroom tiles. I wanted to stay in this shower of hot tears. I wanted the jets to be stronger, the steam to be steamier. I laid myself down in the tub with the hot water still running, and held on to myself in an embrace that wanted to comfort the woman who was so deeply hurt. I wanted to reassure her that she'd be fine.

"You will survive this. You will get over it!"

The Korean woman who had inspired me with her story in Dallas had survived worse circumstances. Her family had rejected her because she was a girl. They had abandoned her … Maybe thinking about her tragedy might help alleviate my distress?

But the outpour of grief was overwhelming. The water was burning hot. Maybe if I burned my skin it would dull the pain in my heart. A very long time elapsed.

When I got back into bed, I touched Jean-Paul on the cheek and passed my fingers through his hair. He looked so distraught. His eyes were red from crying. I almost felt sympathetic. But I was so angry with him I couldn't speak for a while. I was also angry with myself. Wasn't I partly responsible for what had happened? Had my being tolerant in wishing him well in his affair made me an accomplice? Didn't my apparent acceptance of the situation encourage him to have a good time when he was with her? Why didn't I warn him to be careful? But how could I have guessed that they'd be so foolish, so irresponsible? Was it really an accident or had this woman planned it carefully? She must have known very well what she was doing!

Finally I blurted out the question that had crept into my mind: "Have you considered an abortion?"

"She doesn't want to have one."

"Of course not. She is assuring herself of your ever lasting attention by giving you a baby."

Jean-Paul was ignoring my remarks. He wanted me to know what his main concern was:

"I want to be there for her and give the child my name. I also want to send some money every month to help with the expenses."

I barely acknowledged what he was saying. That wasn't my problem.

Jean-Paul appeared to be angry with himself as well as with her for their carelessness.

What caused me the greatest despair was the realization that they would be forever tied to one another. I had to face the fact that even if the affair had ended, the relationship would continue. Should I acknowledge the true feelings in my heart for this woman who had seduced my husband and was now with his child? I desperately wanted to replace the hatred by indifference. But at this stage, I felt a deep resentment. I despised her for having made sure, perhaps unconsciously, but also perhaps with calculating precision, that they would be connected forever.

Hate is not a word I like to use. And right then no word described more accurately the way I felt. I hated this state of affairs. I hated hurting so much. I hated having been betrayed. I hated the idea of having this proof that my husband had a love affair. It was an affair that could have been forgotten. It might have taken years but now that could never happen. Now there would be a constant reminder that would forever drag me back to that reality. This was a burden I feared would be too heavy for me to carry. Yet I also believed that I had this amazing inner strength that would help me overcome any adversity I might face. I was partly responsible for having been too permissive. I had wanted to save my marriage and had decided to give Jean-Paul a sense of freedom, thinking that it would bring us back together. He had come back to me but with a deeper attachment to this woman because of her condition, and with an uncertainty about our future that I found difficult to cope with.

I could not help but think that they secretly wished for this to happen. Both of them. An innocent life was on the way because of their foolishness. The pretense that the relationship was "not very sexual" as Jean-Paul had alluded to in an e-mail was such a joke.

My husband reminded me one more time of his primary concern:

"Do you understand why I've asked you to find a job? I'm going to need some help to support this other family."

I looked at him in utter disbelief. I totally lost control and shouted:

"Stop asking me to make money so that you can support this girl. You're going way too far now. It's her choice to keep the baby. She didn't have to break the news to you if she was as noble as you thought she was! Do you think she has any concern for the damage she is causing to our relationship? Come on! I see the whole plan very clearly now. She's getting you so messed up that I will be forced to leave you and then she'll have you. This is so f … up!"

I hurried to pick up my journal that I had brought to the hotel, as there was something I just had to read to Jean-Paul at that moment.

> *When you say that Efelia reminds you of your mother it hurts me deeply. You know how much I loved and admired your mom. How could you compare her with this adulteress, when it was your mother who had to suffer from your father's infidelities? In all the years since I've known you I've never heard you say that anyone reminded you of your mother. I didn't think any woman could ever measure up to her. So it is really difficult for me to see you compare this woman who has seduced you to your mother. For me it's an insult to her memory.*

Jean-Paul attempted to laugh and I knew that was a sign of nervousness. What I had written had struck a cord. It made him uncomfortable.

"It really hurts me when you laugh about something so serious, you know. It upsets me. I know that you do it to lighten up the mood and to change my state. It irritates me more than it distracts me from the seriousness of the situation when you joke about it. I'm going to need time to adjust to these circumstances."

The friend that Jean-Paul had in me fully understood his torment. The wife was furious, angry and rebellious, especially when she remembered that he has asked several times for some kind of financial help. That was not going to happen. Now more than ever, I would not get a job outside of our home. My reasoning was that we had a comfortable lifestyle. Jean-Paul was overseas to make extra money. If he came back to live at home then I would consider going to work! That was logical, no? My husband called it *logique de cheval* (horse logic).

I thought it made perfect sense. I had worked before. I was in Commercial Real Estate for about five years and spent another three or four in residential sales. Our girls were younger. Their father was not traveling as much. We had a more stable life. I had earned enough money to put a deposit on our first real estate venture in Hawaii. I considered this my participation in our financial partnership. Besides, with all the moves of the past several years, how did Jean-Paul expect me to hold a steady job?

Hearing that the reason he needed me to earn money was because he was going to have to support two families now made me want to hit him. Did I give a damn? Was it my responsibility to earn a salary so that he could support another woman, this new baby and the son she had of another man? I was flabbergasted! Had my husband lost his faculty to be objective about this state of affairs? Once again I was troubled by the thought of what the woman might have used to enthrall him. That would explain the pregnancy. A man as careful as Jean-Paul would not have let this happen. It was unthinkable that she could trap him so easily. I had heard stories about what Venezuelan women did to married men. Now it was happening to my husband. I felt shattered by what this Efelia girl might have done to him. Of course, when I pointed out to Jean-Paul what my suspicions were, he denied vehemently that his friend could have anything to do with any kind of deceptive tactics.

What was foremost on his mind right now seemed to be what his guilt forced him to consider as a top priority. The next time he brought it up, I stopped him:

"Please stop telling me that I must find myself a job. Please! It's really not my problem if you have to support another woman now!"

"I'm sorry!"

"Just never, ever talk to me about this again. Please!"

"Okay. Sorry. I'll never bring it up again. I'd like to tell our daughters about the pregnancy. When do you think I should do that?"

"I would wait maybe 3 or 4 months. She could have a miscarriage, you know! No one needs to know anything now!"

"What about our friends?"

"I'm the one who will talk about this to Dana, she's my best friend. I will probably need to speak to someone who can help me cope!"

"Well, just be careful whom you talk to. You want people who are not going to be judgmental."

"I really don't feel like saying anything to anyone right now. And don't tell me whom I can and cannot talk to about it!"

I cried myself to sleep on that Saturday night and woke up crying on Sunday morning. All the repressed anger, fear and deception I had held back were surfacing. Why couldn't this just turn out to be a bad dream?

I was thankful that there was no one at home on the Sunday when we got back from the Solana hotel. Jean-Paul kept out of the way and Danielle was at work at Just Java. Our friends Nadia and Raoul, who had been staying with us since we had met in Kona were visiting Raoul's mother outside of Dallas. I did not want to see or talk to anyone. I had been deeply wounded. I felt ashamed, deceived and betrayed. I just lied down on the couch in our library and stayed there most of the day. I was unable to read, unable to pray, or even to meditate. My mind was a blur. Thoughts were racing at high speed. The shame, the despair mingled with the thoughts. Something uncontrollable, something that I've read about but never experienced first hand, something was destroying my marriage. Something I couldn't fight, some abyss was engulfing me ...

I thanked God that the love Jean-Paul and I had for one another was as deep as it was. And I hoped that it would survive this ordeal. For the time being, I just wanted to sleep. I wish I had some sleeping pills. I would gladly knock myself out with a few and wake up on another day.

Jean-Paul did all he could to help me improve my state of mind. He held me in his arms and asked for my forgiveness, he told me that he loved me and that he was sorry for all the pain he'd caused me. Eventually, the anger dissipated even if the hurt remained.

I was still having sudden outbursts. After lunch on Sunday, I threw a plate into the sink with enough force to break it. When it didn't explode as I had wanted, I started sobbing uncontrollably and ran to hide in our bathroom until I could regain my senses.

Later that afternoon I began to feel more at peace. When he returned from riding his bicycle, I was able to express to my husband almost all that I had in my heart. I told him how much it hurt me to see him almost happy by his circumstances: he had pointed out to me that the baby would be born in the year 2000. And that it would be something special. He had also said that it made him feel young to be an expecting father again at 53. I wanted to punch him when he said it. He should be thinking about becoming a grandfather, not a new father!

I hoped that the pain I felt would lessen quickly because it was quite unbearable. It also transformed me into this hateful woman I didn't recognize.

Nadia and Raoul returned home on Sunday evening and Jean-Paul asked if he could share his 'secret' with them. Why not, I thought? They were as impartial as we could find. Although we had met them barely one month ago, they had showed a lot of affection to both of us.

I didn't utter a word and allowed Jean-Paul to do the talking. Although wild and unpredictable, Nadia could be quite philosophical at times. After he had told them everything she said to us: "Guys, there is a reason for this happening and you must seek the lesson to be learned."

"I know for sure that I'm learning about humility," I commented. "It's a virtue I've never possessed. I've always bragged about what a great relationship Jean-Paul and I have and now the whole world can see that it wasn't the kind of dream relationship I was describing. If he could cheat on me and seek pleasure elsewhere while being as careless as he's been, and completely lose control of the situation, then our relationship must really have been flawed. Humility, tolerance, forgiveness … I can think of a few lessons this experience is teaching me."

"Jean-Paul, what about you? What lesson are you learning?" Nadia asked.

"I think I'm being given another opportunity to raise a child and use all the material I've discovered in the last few years. I can make a difference in the lives of some people who need my help."

Somehow, this wasn't making much sense to me. Was he thinking of adopting the child? This girl lived in another country, another continent. South America was so foreign to me. We had been to Brazil a couple of times and that was a 10-hour flight from JFK airport, and probably eight or nine from Dallas Fort Worth. It seemed like another world. How would he make a difference in their lives unless he planned on moving there? That was not something I wanted to even consider. He would have to go by himself.

I was tired. I needed to sleep. I had a second glass of red wine at dinner that evening. It would hopefully help me sleep better. Maybe the nightmare would end. Maybe I'd wake up and find out it had only been a bad dream.

7

Life lessons

When Jean-Paul returned to the office on Monday morning I sent him an e-mail in which I thanked him for the early morning treat. He'd made love to me before he left for work. It had been his way of soothing my pain and torment. He'd witnessed how I hadn't been able to control my tears, crying often without warning.

Later, he told me on the telephone that Efelia was besides herself with grief.

"She doesn't have too many people to blame for her condition apart from herself, you know!" I remarked.

I could feel no sympathy for her. I was so upset with both of them. She must have gotten pregnant just a few days before Jean-Paul and I met in Kona.

"She probably knew you'd be breaking up with her and she made sure she caught your child so the two of you would remain connected."

I was overcome by my fury. I was losing my mind. I was remembering Kona and my prayers to God to bless her out of our lives but it had been too late. Efelia had already conceived their baby.

"How can you be sure the child is yours?" I wanted to know.

I worked part time at a new home development near my house in Southlake. The builder's representative came from Venezuela. We worked in the same office. When I confided in him that Jean-Paul was involved with his secretary, Ricardo told me to warn my husband that it was a common occurrence for women from his country to pretend that they were pregnant with an unsuspecting foreigner's baby to obtain their monetary support. I wanted some proof that the child was my husband's.

Jean-Paul was quick to reply:

"I have no doubt that this baby is mine. And I know precisely when it happened."

I was heartsick. I needed time to heal. I needed a friend in whom to confide. But I was too ashamed to call any of my friends and tell them what blow I'd just been dealt.

My husband's love helped me to bear the enormous weight on my chest, the grief, the bitterness, the sorrow. Ironically enough, it was Jean-Paul, the source of my biggest heartache who was helping me carry this heavy burden. I loved him for the affection he showered me with. I would accept this trial as payback for the pain I had caused him when I thought I was in love with another man.

◆   ◆   ◆

Jean-Paul admitted telephoning Efelia daily. I didn't take this news well. What must they talk about? Is he promising her a future in which he plays a part in her life? Will he serve as substitute husband, maybe? I felt that he was so engrossed in her drama that he wasn't seeing things in perspective. He was at home here with me yet a part of him was still in Venezuela. Did I have the capacity to live the rest of my life with this "monster under my bed?"

I needed to get involved in something that would keep my mind occupied. I decided to volunteer my time and I called a Women's shelter to offer my services. I figured that by meeting women in worse situations than my own, I'd tolerate mine better. These were battered women, hiding from partners who mistreated them both physically and mentally. The shelter's location was kept confidential and they only gave me the address when I was a block away from the place. Their secret life became an important part of mine.

I also organized small workshops for my colleagues at the Toastmasters International Club I belonged to. One of those workshops was: "How to rekindle the flame of your romantic relationship." I told those in attendance that the workshop was as much for them as it was for me. Although I didn't share what my situation was, I admitted going through some issues that the workshop might help alleviate.

◆   ◆   ◆

Time is a great healer. What initially seemed insurmountable I'd learned to live with and accept as another life lesson after only a few weeks. The thought of abortion as an option to the situation now seemed like such a horrible thing to do to the little innocent whose life was unwanted yet precious. I knew my husband was suffering. He felt torn between the love he already felt for the baby and his wanting to spare me further pain. As for me, I reassured myself that if that baby was really his, I would be able to love it.

We exchanged some emails.

Jean-Paul,
I understand you wanting to do what's right in continuing to offer your friendship to this girl.
My pride gets in the way. I imagined many scenarios, and none had come anywhere close to this reality.
You ask me to put myself in her shoes, and try to understand why you behave the way you do towards her … Can you put yourself in my shoes and understand my state of mind?
Mia

Mia Darling,
I understand you in your turmoil and I admire your courage to face such devastating news. I know that with time everything will be all right if we focus less on how shameful this is and more on the beauty of life.

I do understand your lack of trust regarding Efelia. I would probably feel the same way if I were you. I actually found myself wondering if she had not done it intentionally. And I quickly realized that I was as much to blame. I could have prevented this from happening. She is a young woman, humble and lonely, who has met her Prince Charming. What willpower could she demonstrate in front of me? I'm the one to blame. I thought about the consequences when it was too late. Maybe I wanted to assure myself of her forever friendship.

Thanks for being so understanding. I know that life will give it back to you. My friendship with Efelia is that of a brother who is helping his less fortunate sibling to design a better future. This baby will remind me of my promise to her. I'm sorry to drag you into my drama. But if I have to face such a trial in my life, no one better than you could help me overcome what awaits me. I kiss you passionately.

JP

Jean-Paul,

I wanted to reassure you about this unborn child's future. You mentioned that you're already concerned that if something should happen to you, what would happen to the child? Know that I would continue sending whatever financial support you had decided upon for the child.

During my morning meditation, this is what I've come to observe:

When we are both totally at peace with our inner selves, when we are doing in our emotional and spiritual lives exactly what we strive to do, then we will experience bliss, and our hearts will reach a state of complete union that exists only once in a lifetime.

Yours, always,

Mia

Later in the week I confided in the friend that I have in my husband that I was in a debilitating state of mind. My moods were spiraling downwards. I was having negative thoughts that I had neither energy nor desire to fight. I was weak in body and spirit. I had allowed other people's point of view to affect how I felt.

Jean-Paul reminded me from time to time that I could change my state of mind in a heartbeat. I just needed to decide to do it. What did I really want? Did I want to continue to suffer from this situation? Or was I willing to do whatever it took to eliminate the negative emotions triggered by our circumstances? We both had attended enough self-mastery seminars to know exactly how to get out of a disempowering mood. When I felt really down, one particular exercise always uplifted my spirits: Listening to a powerful soundtrack from a favorite movie or an instrumental recording, I would "pulverize" an unpleasant situation using a Terminator style machine gun. I wasn't killing anyone. I was just eliminating the situations or the emotions that I wanted to get rid of. After the destruction came the good part. I "showered" myself with the feelings I wanted to experience: peace, love, faith, trust, happiness, while the music resonated inside my head, and found its way into my heart. This process was helping me bring peace and harmony back into the chaos of my life.

I was fortunate to have friends like Nadia and Raoul. They both had come into our lives exactly at a time when we needed unbiased friends who could offer impartial advice. They obviously had been placed on our path for a reason!

Our first-born had also been nonjudgmental and supportive. When Jean-Paul told her of the situation, Chloe wrote to me and offered surprising and uplifting advice. My oldest daughter was becoming a friend and a confidante. I would smile thinking of the difference between the rebel and wild child of 10 years ago and the wise young woman she had become. Chloe had been diagnosed with bipolar disorder when she was 16. She took her prescribed medication for several years. After she graduated from college in Alaska, she was firmly determined not to depend on the drugs all her life. She gradually weaned herself from both Zoloft and Lithium and replaced them with meditation and yoga practice. She successfully overcame a misleading and most probably incorrect diagnosis. Her e-mails were a source of great comfort. She would remind me how proud she was to have me as her mother.

> *Manman chérie,*
> *The pain, the frustration and sense of betrayal that you might feel towards Daddy is emotional toxicity. You know this, and you know that you will have to get yourself in gear and get over this if you ever want to be happy. I know that you will and that it will make you a stronger person. You will grow and learn that any act made with love is a positive step, but it can turn negative without the right follow-through.*
> *You may need to look beyond your feelings and instead perceive this as a lesson in true love, in reaching beyond what you think is expected of you to act in a magnificent, noble way. You are the one who has to make the decision as to whether or not this child will have Daddy as a father figure. It sucks, it's a lot to be put on your plate, but that's the way it is, and now the question is, what are you going to do about it?*
> *I hope you use this experience to propel you closer towards enlightenment and complete self-actualization. Thanks for reminding me that life is simply amazing and it's all about being happy and helping others be happy.*
> *I'm so damn proud of you for being this tolerant, this strong, this open with your feelings. I really am proud to be your daughter.*
> *Much love, and my thoughts are with you,*
> *Chloe*

◆   ◆   ◆

At times, I seemed to be suffering from a split personality disorder. For example, when talking to Jean-Paul, the other Mia wanted to slap and shake me. After speaking to him, I would call myself a liar, a fake and a fool. Why couldn't I be more honest about how I truly felt? Why pretend that I was so strong when in fact I felt weak and powerless? Was it because what Jean-Paul most admired in me was my usual inner-strength? I didn't want to disappoint him by showing my weakness.

No one could fully understand my heart except for myself. I was faced with a difficult choice: truth at all cost even if it meant more hurt, or pretenses that only I knew were pretenses. I strived for truth and total honesty and I trusted in my future with my husband. On one occasion I wrote to him:

> *When I say "I love you no matter what" it doesn't include if you torture or disrespect me. It doesn't mean if you destroy my self-esteem or kill my exuberance but I'm sure you realize that. Our love will survive because it is stronger than ever before. It will survive because I won't let myself be crushed by all the adversity I am facing.*
> *I will always love you.*
> *Mia*

Jean-Paul returned to Venezuela in November and during his absence, we discussed the possibility of my going to Caracas at the beginning of December to meet Efelia. When we first considered it, he spoke of a promise made to her to have a farewell lunch on his last day in Venezuela. He reassured me that he would cancel his engagement with her unless she agreed to meet me.

The only person I confided in about my trip was my friend Dana.

"I need to meet her so I can accept this woman who is expecting my husband's child."

"Are you sure this is what you want to do? Why do you even want to know her?"

"Because Jean-Paul has already decided that he wants to play a part in the child's upbringing."

"Is he thinking of moving to Venezuela?"

"Gosh, noooo, but he might be sent there for his job. I don't know, hon. I just need to go, if only to get rid of the idea I have of her, that she's some kind of a witch that has cast a spell on my husband. I want to find out what she's like. I'm curious, you know!"

I did realize that there was a possibility that Efelia might not want to meet with me but I wanted to travel to Venezuela. We had friends there that I could stay with. And I wanted to find out what it was about this girl that had made my husband lose his head.

The visit might help me to overcome the feelings of doubt, jealousy and envy that I had to fight constantly because I was dealing with the unknown. I asked Jean-Paul to let Efelia know that I had enough compassion and understanding in my heart to forgive her the same way I had forgiven him. Even if deep inside I felt unsure of how I'd react in her presence, I would fly to Caracas for a weekend and meet the woman who was causing me so much heartache. I was ignoring the warnings about the dangerous situation in Caracas: Jean-Paul's company had sent all its employees a list of precautions to take. Robberies were common, even in broad daylight. There were frequent kidnappings and demands for high ransoms. We were told to leave all gold jewelry at home, not to carry expensive pocketbooks and not to drive flashy cars anywhere in the country. People were living in fear. Security was tight everywhere. I would not let these warnings stop me: I would go and find out what we were dealing with. I was praying that I wouldn't live to regret my decision.

8

The reunion

My four days in Caracas were tumultuous. I arrived on a Thursday and spent the first night in San Roman, at our friends Ron and Joanne's stunning 2-level apartment overlooking the city. Jean-Paul was in Morichal, an hour-long plane ride from Caracas, working in the field.

The view was breathtaking from my bedroom window and I tried to imagine where Efelia lived. Jean-Paul had mentioned a humble home in a hilly neighborhood that cars couldn't access. Our friends' apartment building was obviously located in a much more exclusive area of town.

On the way to Ron and Joanne's place I commented that some parts of the city reminded me a bit of Haiti. The contrasts were dramatic between one area and the next. Social conditions of the country are reflected in the disparity of the different barrios.

When he arrived in Caracas from the field on Friday afternoon, Jean-Paul asked me to meet him at the Tamanaco Hotel where we would be spending the next couple of nights. Joanne's chauffeur took us there and said he would come back to pick us up so we could have dinner at our friends' place. Joanne and Ron knew nothing of our situation and we felt more comfortable staying at the hotel, where we would have more privacy.

At first, Jean-Paul seemed happy to see me. When we got to our room I wanted to be in his arms. I wanted his embrace and his kisses. Instead, he barely acknowledged me and made himself busy by checking the stock market on his computer. I made no comments.

I was overcome by uncertainty. My apprehension at meeting Efelia made me nervous. I needed some fresh air, and decided to go for a walk.

When I got to the lobby, however, I remembered the warnings about venturing out on the streets of Caracas alone. It is considered dangerous for *"Gringos"*, in particular. So I remained in the lobby of the hotel and visited its bookstore. I pretended to read a magazine while I fought back the tears. I felt a sense of abandonment and a lack of clarity about why I had come to Caracas, a city I hated so much because of what I associated it with. This was the city where it had all started. It was where all the pain I had experienced these past few months had originated. Why wasn't my husband paying more attention to my needs? Was my trip futile? Was he still in love with her?

I knew that Jean-Paul and Efelia had never actually met at the Tamanaco but it was in a nearby hotel that their affair had taken place and where their baby had been conceived.

Suddenly, I made eye contact with a complete stranger. He was smiling his brightest smile and I smiled back at that handsome young man. "An angel from above", I thought. What a gift his smile had been. He comforted me unknowingly. My tears dried up and I suddenly felt calm and serene.

At that very moment Jean-Paul walked into the bookstore and saw me smiling. He asked me how I felt. "I'm going to be fine," I said.

We walked into the lobby and he took my hand.

"You know, darling, I've been doing a lot of soul searching about the situation. I used to fear that I might die young like my grandfather or my mother. But now I know that I have to be around longer because this baby is my reason to be alive."

I couldn't believe my ears. My thoughts were racing. He only cared about this baby; a baby who belonged to a woman who almost wrecked our marriage. I was beyond upset. I was outraged. Had my husband lost all sense of decency? My interpretation of his statement was that if it were not for the baby his life would not be worth living.

I started to cry. Jean-Paul tried to grab me:

"Don't take what I've said in a bad way!"

In my state of mind this was not what I wanted to hear. I felt horrible. He was suggesting that his wife and his three daughters were not enough of a reason for him to want to live but that this woman's baby was.

I just wanted to run away from this place and go back home. I no longer wanted to meet that woman.

I had to get away from my husband. I was sobbing. I ran into the restroom and let it all out. I locked myself inside one of the stalls, hitting the walls with both hands, and crying so hard a woman asked me if I was all right. I just hollered that I'd be fine! My emotions were bottled up and I had tried too hard to suppress them. The anxiety caused by the prospect of meeting Efelia was coming to the surface.

When I had calmed myself down, I washed my face to remove the big black circles of mascara around my eyes. I didn't want Jean-Paul to see how very upset I was. I went back to our room.

"I'm sorry about my outburst."

"What I said wasn't meant to hurt you in any way. I can understand how you could take what I said the wrong way, but all I'm trying to do is find something good in this situation."

I became agitated when he underplayed what he had said. I told him that I was going completely crazy and felt like jumping out of a window.

As I looked out of our hotel room window something stopped me cold. Right there in front of my eyes was a cross in the distance on top of the Avila Mountain. I wasn't alone in this fight. I felt protected by the cross that was all lit up on the mountain in the crepuscule of Caracas. That cross reminded me of what matters the most. I believe in a life beyond this life and in a dimension greater than the one we experience in this realm. The cross signified salvation to me. It represented the Christ who has died for mankind and has promised us eternal life. With faith everything is possible. I showed the cross in the distance to Jean-Paul and simply said: "This is what saves me from insanity."

My tears had dried out. It was a small miracle of God that I had regained my senses so promptly.

Later on, Jean-Paul admitted that while I was having my crisis he wondered for a moment if this was the woman he knew. He had promised his friend Efelia I would show understanding and compassion. He wasn't so sure anymore.

That evening, after enjoying dinner at Ron and Joanne's apartment, we returned to the Tamanaco. Jean-Paul demonstrated his love for me in such a way that I cried all at once tears of relief, sadness, joy and ecstasy.

◆   ◆   ◆

The meeting was on Saturday afternoon. Efelia had resigned herself to come and meet us at our hotel. I went back to our room after lunch to remove some of my jewelry and the bright red lipstick I feared might be too flamboyant for "a girl of small means" as Jean-Paul had described her.

However, she actually wore more jewelry than me. Her nails were nicely manicured and she wore very tight dark blue pants with a lace down both sides, and a simple white blouse. Her bust was small and my idea of a sculpted body with voluptuous hips and big, firm breasts vanished. There was nothing exotic or Asiatic about her. With a crooked nose, small brown eyes, naturally wavy but sparse brown hair, a high forehead and a wide mouth of nicely aligned teeth and brightly colored lips, she was pleasant looking, not pretty, just like Jean-Paul had told me, just like what I had seen in the pictures he'd shown me. We were the same height, and that was the only thing we had in common. She didn't look pregnant to me although she must have been in her 4th month.

She knew I was watching her, yet she shamelessly smiled at my husband with an adoring look. I could see the love she had for him in the look on her face. I thanked God for giving me the strength I had prayed so ardently for. I was breathing normally. I smiled and I spoke to a woman whom I felt I had every right to despise.

It must be that Efelia was easy to like because as soon as I saw her I offered her a comforting half hug and a cheek-to-cheek which she nearly withdrew from.

She said: "*¡Ay, Dios mío!*" (Oh my God) in a soft voice. She seemed to want to run away and my heart went out to her. She reminded me of a wounded animal. She'd brought her four-years old son, Sergio, with her. He was a welcome distraction for all of us. He endeared himself to me by answering enthusiastically to his mother's question:

"*¿Tú piensas que la Señora Mia es bella?*" (Do you think that Sra Mia is pretty?)

Then Jean-Paul asked: "Prettier than your mother?"

Unsure and uncomfortable with the question, he hesitated so I jumped in: "No one should ever be more beautiful to you than your mother."

It was easy to communicate with Efelia, since Spanish was my second language. She could understand English but we spoke exclusively in Spanish during our meeting.

I searched for what Jean-Paul might have liked in Efelia. She had a softness about her, a gentleness that was surely more important than looks. She seemed to be quiet and submissive. He had been seduced by these traits that I didn't possess.

When he went back to our room to get the camera I took advantage of the fact that I was alone with Efelia to say a few things.

"Thank you for coming to meet me. I know it wasn't easy for you."

"*¡Por favor!*"

"We will be fine. Your friend and I are pretty unique people. We have a very special relationship and have no secrets for one another. I wanted to meet you and get to know you so I could accept your baby into our lives."

I had no place in my heart for hatred. I noticed with delight that my heart already felt lighter. It had opened up to love, acceptance, non-judgment. I felt relief. When Jean-Paul returned with the camera I watched the admiring look that Efelia gave him. I also saw the sadness in her eyes. This was the woman who had been my husband's lover. She was carrying his child. She was obviously still in love with him. And I wasn't freaking out. She was smiling bravely, a wide smile. We sat near the pool in the shade. We talked about our favorite books. I mentioned Deepak Chopra's *Path to Love*, she brought up Eric Fromm's *Art of Loving*. We promised each other to read the books that had impacted our lives.

After an hour or so her young son became restless. Fortunately, at that point, Efelia asked Jean-Paul to let her know when she should leave. She had a gift and a card for him. She handed me a letter that was several pages long and a present I hesitated to accept. Since I had also brought her a small gift, a Thomas Kinkade desk calendar, Jean-Paul told me I couldn't refuse her gift and then expect her to accept mine. Her present turned out to be a gold charm of the Virgin Mary with tiny diamonds all around. After she left, I asked Jean-Paul how a girl of her social condition could afford to buy such an expensive gold charm. He said he had no idea.

He asked me if he could wait for their taxi with them. I was fine with this request. My doubts, my jealousy and the insecurity that had been consuming me had nearly all evaporated since meeting Efelia. She didn't look very threatening.

I went up to our room to read her letter to me. It was well written, in her native Spanish, a moving letter, even poignant at times. She wrote from the heart and without pretense. It seemed genuine. It surprised me that she did not ask for my forgiveness, there was no apology either. Jean-Paul had warned me that she was very proud and I could see it in the way she wrote.

During our visit I had told Efelia that she had to be someone special for my husband to have taken a liking to her. Her letter seemed to confirm my initial impression of her. Or was I being sucked into her manipulative scheme just like Jean-Paul had been?

9

The intention
(Efelia)

The letter:
Caracas, December 2, 1999

Sra. Mia,

I've wanted to send you a note or an e-mail for quite some time, since you found out about me. I just wanted to tell you that I know all the bitterness, despair and sadness I've caused you. Please, believe me when I tell you that I do know. From the very beginning, with Pablo,—that's what we call him here—I knew that I was hurting you, him and also myself. He too knew it, but the feeling was so deep and strong that we couldn't help what happened, even though we tried to avoid it. I don't want you to feel bad, or saddened by what I am saying.

The intention of this letter is to show you that I'm not as bad as you may think. (Of course you have every reason to think so.) I am aware that I was wrong from the very beginning to dare to desire someone who wasn't free. But I never, ever thought of possessing him as if he were an object, or thought of stealing him from you. I simply gave him my love unconditionally, he accepted it, and I gave him all of myself, I gave him what I never gave anyone before. Without hoping for anything in return, without measure, and from the deepest part of my soul. I never asked him to leave anything for me, much less his family of which I know he is very proud.

We were both like an open book. We were very sincere in everything. I believe that this is what led us to fall in love. I don't know you, but I believe you must be a special woman, and I'm glad that things are now better between you two. The truth is I'm feeling more at peace already.

I want to tell you that you too should feel at peace. Once, Pablo spoke of "forgiveness." I asked him: "Forgive what?" The only one who has the power to forgive is our Supreme Creator, God. Because He is the only one who is free of all guilt and all sins. God is who forgives and more so when He knows that it was all done in the name of love. And He has forgiven me already.

Many people speak of forgiveness. Many poets, crazy writers and everybody else speak of forgiveness. I have done so myself many times. When one asks with the soul, with one's heart held in one's hand, with tears in one's eyes, and looking up to the heavens, that is true forgiveness. And yes, it does exist.

It may seem to you that I speak too much. In fact, I would like to say so many things that I've kept to myself, thinking about and hoping to one day have a talk with you. Like two women who would meet somewhere and would start talking to one another.

It's just that I want to say, for example, that you are a very lucky woman to have a husband like Pablo. And also that he's not the one responsible for what happened, nor am I, nor are you either. I always told Pablo that he is not from this planet (I often call him "ET"). He is a fabulous man, with an immense heart, with a unique soul. Once I told him that he was a gift from God. He deserves a lot of affection, tenderness, love and all that a big kid could wish for. At your side, Sra. Mia, Pablo is the happiest man on earth, even though he has known Efelia. He still is eternally in love with his wife. You should never doubt it, and you should be very proud of that. He never was separated from you. He always spoke of an extraordinary woman, loving and also enterprising.

Even though for you I may be the worst woman in the world, let me tell you that I don't see myself as such. I recognize that I have loved Pablo with all my heart and soul, with all the passion in the world, with all my tenderness and my simplicity.

I know that you are a very intelligent woman, that's why I wish to ask you something that may appear daring. Listen to your heart, listen to Pablo, believe in him and in what he tells you. My friend Pablo is not crazy. He is not shameless, like you or others might believe. He is not blind either. Simply we learned to see with our soul and with our eyes closed. He is a fantastic man, a great friend, a pal. Well! You know him better than I do. Do not blame him for what happened. In this case, there is no one to blame. That's just life. These are tests, nothing more. It makes us aware that we are alive.

If ever you were to tell this story to "someone" I'm sure that this "someone" would not understand and would immediately say all the bad, the horrible, the worst and the unspeakable of Pablo and Efelia, and they would ask you: "How could you stand this situation?" They would say that no one should put up with such a situation and they might even "advise" you to do what is expected by our society. Do you know why they would speak so poorly about people they don't know? Sadly Sra. Mia, it is because they don't know what it really means to love someone. They don't know the feeling. And they would think that their mind's only limit is to think. They don't make room for the soul, but it's because they don't know anything of grace, of wisdom, they don't really know what love is all about.

I beg you not to believe all the bad things said about me. I'm not going to take anything from you, Sra. Mia, or from anyone. I am a normal woman, I am not crazy, much less a shameless person. If I were, I wouldn't be writing this letter to you and it wouldn't matter at all what people could think. Your husband wouldn't be with a crazy woman.

When I began to suspect that I might be pregnant, I didn't want to accept it, it was so sad and wonderful at the same time. When I found out the truth, I didn't know how to tell Pablo. I didn't know how to face him. He suffered a great deal and I believe he's still suffering for the hurt he is inflicting upon you and your family.

He gave me the choice to make a decision. I cried a lot and I'm still suffering and crying at night for all the pain I've caused you. But if I had decided not to have the baby, everybody would be pleased and happy but I could never forgive myself. It never occurred to me not to have that baby. I would have had to live with this pain until the end of time, and in silence, which is even worse. I'm responsible for my body, and I love my baby. I feel much better now.

Despite all that has occurred to me in my life I feel capable of coming out ahead. Of course, at first, everything will be difficult, but I have a lot of love in my heart and I will give it to my family, I won't think of anything else. I'm going to obtain what I desire, and I'm certain that I will succeed!

Rest assured that I will not bother you for ANYTHING. I'm not like the women who manipulate men with babies. This is not my style. I've always worked. I don't like for anyone to give me anything. I'm not interested.

Don't let what I'm saying bother you. I'm simply being quite honest with you. I know why you came to Venezuela. There are many reasons, I know, but the main reason was to see where your husband has been all this time, and with whom. Don't worry. I understand perfectly well. This too is LOVE.

My intention, with this letter, with these words, is to give you some peace of mind, and to ask you not to let yourself be influenced by people, by those who called themselves "friends." A friend gives advice with uplifting words, and doesn't entertain doubts, or put more fuel to the fire.

A friend helps to calm the storm, many times he or she just listens, and doesn't provoke more uncertainty. Trust in yourself, in what your heart tells you, in the immense love you have for your husband and your family. Have faith in Pablo. He deserves this opportunity. Don't doubt anymore. Above all, have faith in God. He will never forsake you. We are all entitled to having another chance, we all have made mistakes, some bigger than others.

I must say this to you: can you think of a time in your life when you said something that caused pain to someone? Think of that time for a moment. If this ever happened, do you realize that you were forgiven, and that the person gave you another opportunity?

Sometimes, we forget to see with our eyes closed, and to say to those we love how much we love them. They know it, but it's nice to hear it from time to time. To let them know that they are very dear to us. Sometimes the routine makes us forget the delight, the beauty and the magic of love. Do not let this happen with your family. I'm not the one who should tell you what you need to do because you have more wisdom than me. But I appreciate Pablo and all that makes him happy, and that includes you.

I just want for you to feel once again the trust, the love, and all the passion and the tenderness in the world towards Pablo. He too wishes this to be. I understand it, I know it. We are friends of the heart. I'm able to understand many things, as difficult as they are, and even more so when they concern someone as wonderful, as fantastic, and as sincere as Pablo. Give him your trust one more time, and all your love. Like always. Please give him your unconditional love.

Do not worry about anything. I will not bother you two. I will be fine. I hope so. I have faith in myself and I await excitedly the birth of my new baby. This fills me with joy. It is wonderful, it fills all the empty spaces that my heart could have. My two children are my greatest love. They are a dream for tomorrow, and my most precious treasure. Right now, I feel very sad but I know that the nostalgia I feel will disappear slowly. I don't know when I will heal, it may be years. I don't know that I will ever be able to love this way again. The only important thing is that I am at peace with God and also with myself. And I hope that you will find peace also.

I'm sorry that this letter is so long. But I hope that it has helped you have more certainty and also to know me better. I've told you what was most important and there is a lighter feeling in my heart.

I wanted to wish you both all the best, from the bottom of my heart. Be extremely happy. Love Pablo very, very much, like before. And make him feel like the happiest man in the world, just like it used to be. Love him for both of us. For you and for me. Because both you and I are very fortunate women. You, of course, more than myself because you are his wife, and I for having been so fortunate as to have known a man like no other, a unique, an extraordinary human being who for a while filled with joy, love and magic the life of a lonely girl. He has left me with beautiful things that I would not exchange for all the gold in the world. He gave me hope, faith and courage to continue to move forward. This is who Pablo is. Unique. To know him has been a "gift from God and from whoever is looking at us from above, those who watch us from beyond the stars." (I often told him this).

Remember, Sra. Mia, Pablo is neither crazy nor shameless. You would not be with a crazy man, would you? (Smile) Me neither. I'll go now and I hope that my words have helped you feel better, more at peace, happier, more sure of yourself, and more loved. If I have said anything that bothered you, the intention was to be very honest with you and to help you know who Efelia really is. She is not the bad woman that everyone may think she is, and forgive me for what I'm saying: these people who think so poorly of me, they don't have a heart that is anything like mine. They do not know what love is all about. What a shame!

You are different, don't do like your "friends." I think that the best friends that you can count on are yourself, your family and of course God. You are a clever woman and I am sure that you can listen to your heart.

Goodbye, Sra. Mia.

I wish you all the best. Show your love to Pablo the way he shows his for you. You both deserve it. Excuse me if I've been hard in my letter but I know that we will be more at peace from now on.

Sincerely,
Efelia

PS: If you feel that you'd like to say anything to me, you can do so with confidence, and without fear. Thank you so much for "listening" to me. This is the first time that I have written such a long letter to anyone.

10

Tribulations

The next few months were spent alone in Southlake. Danielle was in college at the University of Texas in Denton and Jean-Paul in Venezuela. I was keeping myself busy reading, listening to uplifting music and books on tape, and confiding in the very few friends I could trust would be supportive. Unexpectedly, a friend I hadn't heard from in at least 8 years reappeared in my life like an angel sent from heaven right when I was looking for a shoulder to lean on.

Delphine was a very dear friend of ours. She had been married to Jean-Paul's cousin. After her divorce, we lost touch when she remarried a man several years her senior and moved to Florida. Was it mere coincidence that she got my e-mail address through a mutual acquaintance when I most needed her unbiased, loving advice? Our correspondence helped me get clarity about many of the issues I was facing. The renewed friendship was truly a blessing.

We exchanged several e-mails. I once commented to her that the relationship with Efelia could have ended in a worse manner: she could have given Jean-Paul AIDS, for example, or he could have died of a heart attack while in bed with her! I had learned years ago that when you face a problem, you should think of how much worse it could be. This way you would begin to appreciate how insignificant it was in comparison! I wrote to Delphine:

> *This situation is an incredible test to my ability to keep my dignity as well as my sanity. I do have faith in our future, however. I know God's grace*

will manifest itself and that I'll be blessed with the strength, courage, endurance and resilience necessary to keep my head up high. I take long baths in my Jacuzzi, indulge in relaxing massages and read uplifting material to remain centered, serene and sane.

Delphine's answer:

Dear, dear Mia,

Thank God you are doing the right things: praying, pampering yourself, and letting your better nature win over. I am touched that you have opted to behave like a lady, a loving, understanding wife, an enlightened person in this world where it is so easy to let a problem become misery.

Everything can be a blessing or a punishment depending on how you look at it. We have been raised with a set of values and a perspective that don't allow for natural things to be considered natural. We have twisted life around to fit our selfish needs and in the process we have forgotten who we really are.

But you, Mia, have heart. You know what matters. The proof is in the graceful way you held yourself in the face of circumstances that would make any woman go crazy. You were able to talk to the woman, give her a gift and receive one from her. You were able to forgive your husband. You have grown so much.

I am sure that even though you are hurt and feel tremendous conflict within, there is also a tremendous peace that has come over you with the acceptance of the situation. That is priceless. That is the Truth. That is the feeling you must hang on to because the core of the matter is, no one belongs to us. No situation is secure. But once you have opened your heart truly and sincerely, the love that fills it up, no husband, no lover, no marriage can ever replace. This is what you take with you to the grave. That's the measure of a human being. Hang on to that love that forgives all and your pain will go away.

My wish for you both is that this seemingly awful situation turns into a

most wonderful blessing for all involved. When we keep the faith and give
our life to what is most sacred within us, things do have a way of working
in the most amazing way.
I love you, I am with you, I pray for you.
Delphine.

In addition to Delphine, our daughters were also a constant source of comfort. After giving Chloe the news, Jean-Paul had also told Suzanna when she visited us during Spring Break. She had offered moral support, reassuring me that my mental toughness would help me overcome this crisis. With Danielle, who was living at home with me, it had been more difficult. Jean-Paul wanted to tell her in person. He was away most of the time. She was in school and working a part-time job. When he finally told her, she burst into tears. She had seen me in some of my lowest moments. I had not wanted to discuss with her the reason for my sadness. She was angry at her father. She told him what he had done was stupid. At least we could now talk about it and she too was very supportive of me and showing more indulgence when I was suddenly morose or acting like a nervous wreck! I was really fortunate that our daughters were all three such pillars of strength and were so loving and supportive while we were going through our crisis!

◆   ◆   ◆

A suggestion I found in the book *The Art of Resilience* by Carol Orsborn was to ask myself the question: "Is there any chance that I am taking things a bit too seriously right now?" This was a great question to snap me out of a debilitating state of mind! The book also offered a prayer that inspired me to write my own:

"God, I ask you to use me.
Take my fears, my arrogance, my failures, my ignorance,
and use me to serve those on my path.

In sadness or in joy. In hatred or in love.
Use me Lord. Use me in any way."

I would repeat this prayer often, and keep the focus on these words also found in the book: "Remove the obstacles that separate you from divine love. Open yourself to the unbounded joy of the universe, and stand before the mystery of divine love in awe and reverence. Relinquish the expectation that you will get things back to the way they were. You must be willing to be profoundly changed."

◆   ◆   ◆

The last holiday season of the century was saddened by the death of Mamita. Jean-Paul, Danielle and I were on our way to Maui when my brother Maurice delivered the news to us at the Honolulu airport. Our mom's sisters whom we called Mamita and Mamiline had played the role of grandmothers to our children and Mamita had been a second mother to me even while my mom was still alive. I had often wondered how she would react to our news. I wanted to wait until I would see her. I knew she'd understand. She had a heart of gold. She loved babies. She had not been feeling well lately and had decided not to join us in Maui for this holiday season. Mamiline had traveled alone this time, which was unusual.

Neither one of the sisters had children of their own. My mom had given them nine nephews and nieces and our children were their grandchildren. I knew my siblings were all devastated by Mamita's passing. Even though she had been hospitalized recently, the news was quite shocking to all of us. We had been hopeful her health was improving since she was to be discharged in just two days.

That evening we gathered to pay tribute to Mamita. My brothers and their wives, my sister and her daughter, Jean-Paul, Danielle and I wanted to celebrate Mamita's life and express our gratitude for all that she had represented for us. The funeral would be in Haiti and none of us were able to attend. We all agreed that she would not like to see us cry. We all adored our auntie. We would miss her dearly. She was truly the most loving, self-less, generous person I knew. In addition, our Mamita had known what it was like to be in an illicit relationship. He was married. She was his secretary. That was a very long time ago. Her story had always intrigued me. She had remained friends with not only his wife but their children as well. Rumor had it that the wife knew everything. Even though it was wide-spread knowledge, Mamita never discussed her 'secret' with anyone. Talking to her might have helped me shed some light on my own confusion and come to terms with my internal conflict.

It took me a few days before I could let the grief express itself. I waited until I could be alone at one of my favorite spots in the area, a lovely beach between Wailea and Makena, near the Prince Hotel. It would be deserted at sunset. We had attended a wedding at the nearby century-old church a few years before. Mamita had been there. I felt her presence very strongly. She always loved the ocean very much. I sat on the hot sand to mourn her in the solitude of this private beach. Mamita's passing was helping me put things in perspective. It somewhat alleviated the intensity of the upset related to the upcoming birth of my husband's child. It placed it in second place. Actually I moved it to third place when I started thinking about other situations that had recently shaken my world.

I remembered our youngest daughter's bout with depression. Danielle was 16 years old when she was first diagnosed with this devastating illness. Even after having dealt with Chloe's bipolar disorder a few years earlier, I had not detected any signs in our last born that would indicate the slightest mental unbalance. Yet, she had ended up three times in the hospital in the past two years. The first time was after scratching her left arm with a dull knife about 20 times, swallowing a whole bottle of pain killers and calling 911 for help. There was some blood on her bedroom floor carpet, when we returned home on that Sunday night, and a note from the police stating that they had answered an emergency call at our home!

Danielle was taken by ambulance to John Roberts Hospital in Fort Worth where she needed to have her stomach pumped. I had wanted to scream and holler and felt as if my insides had exploded when the officer explained that Danielle would be kept under observation because she had tried to kill herself. Not my beautiful "feeling fantastic" daughter! This was what she used to answer when asked how she was: "I'm feeling fantastic!" Jean-Paul and I were stunned and absolutely shocked. I was thankful that she had called 911 for help and that I wasn't alone. Jean-Paul worked in Houston at the time, and he often left Southlake on Sunday night. That weekend he had decided to wait until Monday morning to drive the four hours to Houston. I had gone down on my knees in thanksgiving and put Danielle on prayer chains from Haiti to Hawaii. I thanked God that she was alive. This incident had alerted us to the fact that our youngest daughter was in need of medication for the "acute clinical depression" we didn't even know she suffered from.

She was put on Paxil first, then on Effexor when the symptoms of depression continued. There had been weekly visits to a male psychiatrist she didn't relate to, then to a female psychotherapist who seemed to help until Danielle broke up with her boyfriend Trevor. That breakup pushed her into a catatonic state.

I had to call a neighbor to help me bring Danielle downstairs from her bedroom: she had completely shut down, didn't utter a word for days and was barely able to walk. I took her directly to Charter Hospital at the recommendation of her psychotherapist. They kept her there several days. At least one week. And for an entire month, she went to Charter during the day to attend school and have some much needed therapy. Jean-Paul in the meantime was in Venezuela and considering his next assignment in Nigeria. He was in complete denial in front of the situation when I called to tell him about Danielle's newest bout with depression. When he came home after her stay at Charter, he told the group therapist:

"No daughter of mine suffers from depression. I left a beautiful, normal and healthy daughter. And that's what I see."

It had not been easy going through these challenging times alone, yet I had survived!

The third time Danielle stayed overnight at the hospital was after a breakup with another boyfriend. We would later find out that her fear of abandonment that stemmed from our frequent relocations was at the root of Danielle's bouts with depression.

Although she was living on campus with a roommate at the time, Danielle had a key to our Southlake residence. She had climbed on the roof of our two-story home to hide from the police. We were both in Venezuela at the time and only found out about the incident when we came back to sell the house, right after Suzanna's graduation from Penn State.

Danielle explained the broken kitchen door to us, providing very little explanation as to what exactly had taken place. She was wearing a scarf around her neck and I could see some scars which she told me were self-inflicted. First it was the arm, this time the neck. This tendency to self mutilation had also been present in her sister Chloe. It disturbed me. After this last incident, I had asked myself: "Why can't I be where my daughter needs me, right here in Texas? Why do I have to follow my husband to this god forsaken country I hate?"

I was torn: I couldn't let him go to Venezuela alone. It would seem like I was giving up on him. The baby was expected any day now. He would want to be there. My place was where my youngest needed me. It was also next to my husband.

One early morning while we were in Southlake, Jean-Paul started dialing 011 to place an international call. He hit 911 instead. The police was at our door in what seemed like seconds. One of the men dispatched had been there the night of the roof incident and asked how our daughter was doing. I got the story from him: When the police was alerted by the boyfriend that Danielle was despondent and could potentially hurt herself, they broke down the kitchen door and searched the entire house. Her car was in the garage. They couldn't find her anywhere. As they were getting ready to leave, one last flashlight inspection revealed her silhouette near the chimney. They called the firemen who lowered her to safety with a harness. They kept her under observation at the hospital. Her friend Michelle took her back to her apartment the following day. I allowed gratitude to fill my heart when remembering how we had all gotten over the ordeal Danielle's illness had put us through.

The one thing that most helped me during these trying times was prayer. I was blessed with a strong faith in the power of prayer. And I now had a new angel praying for me: Mamita had joined the spirit realm and she would be watching over me. I would call on her in my hours of despair.

◆   ◆   ◆

Jean-Paul and I were being transferred to Venezuela because of his job. It was a very challenging experience for me. How would I react when the baby came in just couple of months? I was grateful for the values I held, as a result of the education I had received, the books I had read, the philosophers, mentors and teachers I had learned from all these years. Thanks to these values, I was able to rise above my circumstances, and no matter how devastating the situation appeared to be, I could always find within me the strength and the determination to deal with it. I valued my happiness, my peace of mind, harmony and serenity. I nurtured resilience, courage, fearlessness and integrity. My mother had instilled in me the need to always forgive others. So it came naturally to me. It brought solace to my state of mind. And above all, there was the gratitude. I was living in a constant state of gratitude.

Before we left Dallas, I visited a couple of psychotherapists. I wanted advice on how to cope when I'd be physically close to the situation I most wanted to avoid: the birth of my husband's and his ex-lover's child. They pointed out that I was already doing well. They offered to prescribe some anti-depressant "just in case." I declined. I would continue to keep the focus on what was great in my life, and tackle the situation with my own coping tools.

Both analysts asked me what was helping me bounce back so quickly. I mentioned the seminars on self-mastery, the workshops, the coaching. I understood that many relied on tranquilizers or alcohol to help dull their pain. I briefly considered going that route myself. I was very fortunate that prayer, meditation and mental toughness worked well enough for me.

◆   ◆   ◆

Our new home in Venezuela was near the coastal city of Puerto La Cruz, in a pueblo called Lecherias. It was a four-hour drive from Caracas and I was grateful for the distance between Efelia and us. Our building stood only a few feet from the ocean and it afforded us a magnificent view of the bay, the marina and the city of Puerto La Cruz. From the balcony of our 10th floor apartment we enjoyed a million dollar view thanks to the floor to ceiling sliding glass doors, serving both our bedroom and the vast living room. Elegant yachts, some more imposing than actual homes built right alongside the bay; sailboats varying in size from 20 to 60 feet, and dozens of *lanchas,* as the Venezuelans call their speedboats were parked in the marina of El Morro. Our complex was home to several marinas and boatyards and was a popular cruise destination. This area reminded me of the South of France, or the South of Spain. I loved our new residence, even though I did not like the circumstances that had brought me there. Being near the ocean always invigorated me.

I had suffered several setbacks since meeting Efelia due to the fact that Jean-Paul continued to enjoy a close friendship with her. They continued to speak on the telephone almost daily. He had started sending her the financial support she pretended not to want from us despite my suggestions that he should wait until the baby was born.

Finally one day I just had to ask: "Don't you find it a bit premature to be sending her money already?"

"I have promised her to take care of her medical expenses. I feel responsible."

The resentment I felt had become uncontrollable. Insult was being added to injury. Now he had to support her by sending her money? The voices in my head were calling her his mistress, even though I knew there was no longer any physical contact between them. The fact that he was sending her money entitled her to the label.

Was it not possible that his secretary had played her cards so adroitly that the pregnancy looked like an accident when, in fact, she'd engineered the entire episode to benefit from his financial generosity?

I just had to ask the same question that had been playing on my mind for months: "Will you have a DNA test when the baby is born?"

"Why? You still doubt that this baby is mine? Didn't I tell you I know when it happened?"

"Never mind. I simply find it a little strange that she should be so careless, when it has happened to her once before. The woman must have known exactly what she was doing!"

Jean-Paul ignored my remarks. Or, at least, he wasn't commenting and I was left wondering.

Of course he would never abandon a woman who was carrying his child. But what if it wasn't even his baby? I continued to entertain this thought, with the hope that there had been a mistake. I wished the nightmare would end; that I wouldn't have to live with this situation for the rest of my life.

Jean-Paul was harboring a huge amount of guilt because of what had happened. The money was one way to process his guilt. The amount he wanted to send her every month was clearly excessive. It made me resent the situation even more. Doubt, insecurity and fear of an uncertain future for us overwhelmed me.

One of the books that I found helpful at the time was *Secrets About Life Every Woman Should Know*, by Barbara De Angelis:

Her Secret #6 reads: "Make Your Courage Bigger Than your Fear. Fear will steal your Aliveness." That applied to my situation. I had always prided myself on being fearless. Yet since Jean-Paul's confession about his affair, I had let this emotion invade my psyche. I welcomed the advice Ms. De Angelis gave on how to conquer that fear. I developed a new mantra: "I am not my fear. I am magical, spiritual, courageous." I knew that the fear would go away when I stopped feeding it. Courage would replace it. Love would erase it.

The taste in my mouth was that of bitterness, of deception and, at times, of disgust. What helped me keep my sanity was to know deep inside that despite it all, my husband still loved me very much. It was demonstrated in the way he treated me. When he looked into my eyes and reassured me that he could never leave me or be without me, I could believe him. I had faith in him. My journals helped me express my inner feelings:

A disturbing ache stirs my insides when I think of what he has done. I share his responsibility because of my level of tolerance. I barely react in his presence when he confides in me. I pretend to take it lightly, like a good friend would. And that's the role I play: that of a friend. He has become emotionally involved; he has betrayed me in the worst possible way, by fathering a child with a woman he admits having fallen in love with. I become despondent when I think of what awaits me when the child is born. I dig an imaginary hole, deep inside which I bury myself away from the reality I want to escape.

◆　　　◆　　　◆

I was feeling old. I'd be turning 50 in a few months. And even though many said I didn't look my age, when I saw my reflection, I saw the face of an older woman. There was an unfamiliar sadness in her look. Would I ever be able to move on with my life? I thought of what had happened right before we came to Venezuela and how my positive expectation had been vacuumed right out of my heart.

We were ready to move to Puerto La Cruz for this new assignment. Jean-Paul had to leave a few days before I was ready to travel. He promised me that he would not meet with Efelia when he stopped over in Caracas for one night on his way to Puerto La Cruz.

The day after he'd left, he wrote me an e-mail in which he casually mentioned that he had met Efelia in the lobby of his hotel so she could pick up a gift for her son and some vitamins he had brought for her.

I wanted to strangle him! I didn't want him to see her pregnant. She would surely stir old feelings in him looking all cute and vulnerable in her expecting state. I felt disrespected because he had not only broken his promise that he would not meet with her, but because of the very casual way in which he told me about it. It upset me that Jean-Paul could be so callous. I was fuming.

At that time, I was using the services of my Life Coach and friend Miriam. During our next session she asked me after noticing my anger:

"What do you really want?"

"Respect. I want to be respected by my husband, not lied to, not treated the way he's treating me."

"What else do you want?"

"I want to be able to trust him again."

"What else?"

"I want to stop feeling so insecure, so hurt, so unhappy"

"Have you considered the possibility of separating from him?"

"Not really. But right now, I am starting to contemplate it."

"How does that prospect make you feel?"

"Frankly, the humiliation I feel because of how I'm being treated could not be worse than a separation."

That was the first time I had considered that possibility and I thanked Miriam for helping me realize that I would rather be alone than be treated with such lack of respect by my husband.

I cancelled my scheduled trip to join him in Venezuela. I refused to communicate with him for two days, by phone or e-mail. I wondered if he wanted me to leave him so he could be alone in Venezuela. I spent two days at the malls doing some major damage to his credit cards. I was having a shop-till-you-drop attack of sorts. It was more like a spend-till-you-break-free spree.

He did apologize when I finally accepted his calls, admitting he had acted stupidly. I resigned myself to get on a plane and join him in Puerto La Cruz after he reassured me that he was sorry for his lack of judgment.

The day before I was scheduled to leave, however, I suddenly became violently ill. I even feared for my life. Coincidentally, for the first time I was wearing the gold medallion surrounded by tiny diamonds Efelia had given to me when we'd met in Caracas.

I developed the worst sounding cough I'd ever had, and I could barely breathe between coughing spells. It felt as if my lungs were filled with fluid. I imagined a hole in my chest area and when I inhaled, the breathing lost itself into this bottomless space inside me. It petrified me. I simply could not catch my breath. The first thought that came to mind was: "Someone is trying to hurt me!" It triggered the notion of voodoo dolls and evil power. Was I being attacked? Again? Only a few weeks before, I had nearly crushed the tip of my fingers in our electric garbage disposal. I was distracted while trying to find out why it wasn't properly functioning. I flipped the switch ON while my hand was touching the blades! What saved the hand was the fact that the disposal's mechanism shut itself down in that exact instant and refused to start again. The repairman I called couldn't explain how the disposal had locked itself in such a timely manner.

I had a minor car accident right around the same time. I blamed it on my being lost in deep thoughts while driving, as I had a lot on my mind.

A major leak at home from a burst water-heater in the attic had caused serious damage to the ceilings and walls of both floors. I was thinking: "When it rains, it pours." Danielle had commented:

"Mom, someone must be trying to get to you!"

Not until this new incident with the awful cough had I given any attention to how many instances of "attacks" there had been.

I rushed to Dr. Cheng, my acupuncturist, and he treated me for over an hour in his office. He administered finely ground watermelon seeds mixed with boiling hot water, tiny homeopathic pills and bitter Chinese herbs. He applied suction cups on my chest and back as well as the hair-thin needles connected to electric current, and put me under a heating lamp for a good half hour. He suggested that I should go to a hospital if, by the next day, my condition hadn't improved. I had never seen Dr. Cheng as concerned as he appeared to be on that visit.

The cavernous cough continued for days and I had to wear a surgical mask especially around children, just in case I was contagious. The day after my visit to Dr. Cheng, I boarded a plane to Caracas and wore the mask during most of the 4 ½ hour flight. The coughing persisted. My breathing, however, was back to normal. The visit to the hospital was not necessary. The episode did scare me and left me wondering.

Where had I read this article about negative energies that are sometimes carried by stones, especially diamonds? Could those stupid diamonds have held some kind of evil power that was attacking me?

I was also remembering the story of my friend Ana Teresa who lived in Jamaica with a man who had used a piece of jewelry she swore had slowly eaten up at her spirit and turned her into a passive, weak and unmotivated soul. She declared to me that the necklace she never took off because of its great beauty was responsible for her lack of motivation and total dependency on that man.

One day, after her cousin remarked to her how she had become a different person, one with little willpower, drive or ambition, Ana felt as if the necklace were suffocating her and she took it off. She noticed how her companion had looked at her bare neck with unusual intensity but he never made any comment. She had regained her *joie-de-vivre* and her vitality had returned. They had since separated and Ana never wore the pendant again. I was thinking of her story now. I could not intellectually accept such theory as fact, yet why did I get so sick on the very same day I wore the pendant Efelia had given to me? I could find no explanation for this sudden attack other than black magic. My superstition had been fed by early beliefs ingrained from a childhood spent in Haiti where this sort of things was a daily reality. Even though her letter might have indicated otherwise, Efelia's intentions towards me suddenly seemed menacing.

◆　　　◆　　　◆

My best friend in Venezuela was Soraya. We walked on the beach every morning and spoke for hours about our lives. She was one of the few people in Venezuela I confided in. I told her about the diamond pendant and the sudden, unexplained illness. She was alarmed:

"Girlfriend, I don't like what you're telling me, or the way you look. You don't smile anymore."

It was true. I had bouts of insecurity and jealousy, especially when I'd catch my husband in a lie about whom he was speaking to on the telephone, for example. Or when I would find in his attaché case, some old letters Efelia had written to him. Once I made a scene because he refused to let me read those letters. When I accused him of still being in love with her, he reluctantly let me see the letters, but with a promise not to tell his friend that I had read them. He seemed to always want to protect her, to spare her. The uncertainty, the doubt, and the suspicion that arose from his lack of honesty were slowly eating up at what was left of my self-esteem. The negative and debilitating emotions kept resurfacing. Yet I would hide my feelings, afraid to let him see I was no longer the self-assured woman I used to be.

I decided to seek the help of the spiritual healer I had met in Hawaii a few years prior. The private sessions with Marianna had been greatly recommended by a friend of mine. We met in San Diego where I was attending a leadership seminar.

"How can I help you feel better?" she asked with a loving smile at the first consultation.

I expressed my fury and anger to her. She did some muscle testing with a series of homeopathic pills and I observed how my emotions rose to a peak and then slowly dissipated. Marianna administered several natural remedies to address the specific areas where I needed help and I swallowed one tiny Chinese pill after another with some water.

"Express the anger you feel. Use your fists as if you were punching, use your feet as if you were kicking. Imagine the people you want to speak to and let them know how you feel right now."

Marianna was spraying what turned out to be rubbing alcohol while doing her healing. She was also keeping a distance between us, away from my energy field. I was screaming all kinds of insanities and spoke of my hatred, my hurt, my disgust and my despair. I used many four-letter words I didn't even know were in my vocabulary. I felt possessed by an uncontrollable rage then I suddenly regained my composure and felt surprisingly calm.

Marianna's voice was soothing:

"Touch with your hand the area of your body where you feel the most discomfort right now. Is it the chest area, your neck, your shoulders, your stomach?" It was lower, it was the bladder area, where I felt the beginning of an infection maybe. When I touched my lower abdomen, Marianna commented:

"The feeling of betrayal that you're experiencing is in direct relationship with the bladder. It's not surprising that it is where you feel the most discomfort. The emotion is tied to the pain."

"I want you to meditate more and to surround yourself with divine light and with divine love. In order to heal, you need to completely let go of your fears. Surrender to a Higher Power."

Once I had released the burden that was weighing heavily on my heart, once I had cut the cord again and again, there was a sense of inner peace, of relief, of serenity. I was mentally detaching myself from Jean-Paul, so I would no longer feel hurt by his behavior. I experienced a feeling of freedom after the process.

I didn't know how long these new feelings would be with me. I hoped they would remain forever!

At the very end of our session, Marianna put me in a semi-hypnotic state and asked me if I'd ever gone back to a past life. No? She'd lead me.

"Close your eyes. Go back in time to when you were not even born to this life yet. Who are you? Where do you live? Who are your parents? What do you do for a living? What are you wearing? What kind of shoes?"

My answers fascinated me since they came from me yet I had no idea why I was even giving these answers to her. I was from the South of Spain, Sevilla. My mother was a dancer. I had a slight foot defect that prevented me from dancing. I sold pastries. My parents were not married. Marianna took me to the end of that life.

"What have you learned from that lifetime? What do you want to tell the other humans?"

This is what I wrote in my journal right after our session, as my reply to Marianna:

We are instrumental in allowing the events that occur to us. We have within us the amazing power of choice. It's all about choice. It's all about love. Love is the only thing that matters.

Back in Puerto La Cruz I kept myself busy with Latin dance lessons, daily walks on the beach and regular swimming either at the pool of El Faro complex where we lived, or in the ocean waters of El Morro, a short walk down from the pool area. I exercised on my balcony or on the beach near the marina, learned Italian with a 12-cassette program, read avidly and wrote letters to my long distance friends to share my life in Venezuela with them.

I was feeling emotionally stronger every day when I started wondering why I was becoming physically ill so often. I thought there might be something in the food I was eating or in the water I was drinking because on several occasions, I had suddenly become quite violently ill.

Horrible stomach cramps would overcome me without any warning. One night I was on the telephone with Mamiline and I was interrupted in mid-sentence by a painful jolt in the abdomen. I handed the phone to Jean-Paul while I got into a fetal position on the floor in excruciating pain. When Jean-Paul explained that I was having a painful attack, Mamiline said I needed some blessed holy water to chase the bad spirits that were attacking me. I could barely breathe, because of the intensity of the pain.

I asked some of my friends and the local pharmacist what they thought might be causing these sudden attacks and they said it might be the water. We purchased bottled water so I was not sure why I was the one getting sick and not my husband.

One day, I called Dana in Toronto and told her of these sudden, painful attacks. I confided in her about some of my fears.

"Dana, I know you don't believe in spells or curses, but I come from a different culture. And Venezuela is a place where people have beliefs similar to those we have in Haiti. It's not uncommon to cast a spell on someone. I'm not sure it is the case here but I'm a bit alarmed."

"Have you discussed this with Jean-Paul?" she wanted to know.

"I already know what he would say. Of course I can't mention anything to him! But I've never been as sick as I have these past few months. You know that I'm usually in excellent health. Now, without any warning I get these sudden disempowering attacks, it's quite bizarre."

"Honey, you're scaring me. What do you think it is?"

"I just don't know what to make of it. At times I wonder if his friend has used some voodoo tactics to attract him into her web and whether she's using more of the same on me to make me sick."

"Do you want to come and spend some time here with us?"

"No, I just want to confide in you. At times, I feel totally incapacitated. Jean-Paul doesn't believe in that sort of thing. I don't want to believe in it either. I'm just preoccupied."

"Mia, do you think you should even be in Venezuela? Maybe you should go back to Houston."

"No. I'll be fine. I just have my reservations about this girl. I don't know her very well, you know. Anyway, I made Jean-Paul promise that he will never be with her again, even if something should happen to me! So there, if she kills me, she won't have him anyway." I laughed while saying this to her but Dana wasn't amused.

"I don't like what you're telling me. Are you sure you don't want to come and visit us here for a while?"

"I'll be fine, honey. I'm protected by an army of angels."

11

The addition

Toward the end of April, Jean-Paul asked me if Efelia could come to Puerto La Cruz to give birth the following month. I wondered how he could be so obtuse as to not understand how difficult the situation already was for me. I wanted more distance between this woman and us; he wanted her in the same town where we lived when the baby came! That was out of the question! Maybe she had suggested it herself. That didn't seem like something Jean-Paul would think about on his own. I simply replied:

"I wouldn't worry about it, darling. Your friend will do what she knows is best for all of us."

He never brought it up any more.

From my journal:

Sabrina Dora was born on May 20, 2000 when we traveled to Penn State for Suzanna's graduation "Magna Cum Laude." I am grateful that we were away when baby was born. And I am grateful it is not a boy. I silently rejoice and thank God: I don't think I could stand it if it had been a boy.

And to Jean-Paul, in a card I gave to him dated May 23, 2000:

Because she is of you I shall love and accept your daughter into our lives. I am amazed at my level of tolerance, due to the circumstances. God has been good to me. He's given me the fortitude He knew I'd need at this time. Sabrina and her brother will be our adopted children—at least

while we are in this country.
Love, always,
Mia

Jean-Paul expressed the desire to visit his newborn daughter by himself and he went to Caracas when the baby was only two-weeks old. He told me later that he had felt much tenderness in his heart for his infant daughter and also for the mother on that day. He had a moment of weakness, when he held Efelia in an embrace, demonstrating to her that he still cared about her. He had also filmed the baby so I could see her on a video.

When she called to thank me for allowing him to come and meet the baby by himself, it was at the same time strange and almost normal to be speaking to her on the phone. Had I known about the moment of weakness he later brought up, I might not have been as friendly as I was during that phone conversation. When I asked him why he didn't tell me right away, Jean-Paul said he didn't think I would have taken it calmly. He was right.

I was thankful when Jean-Paul could confide in me without my feeling betrayed. It was obvious that he trusted my ability to understand and forgive.

From an entry in my journal:

July 3, 2000
Jean-Paul and I drove to Caracas for me to meet Sabrina this past weekend. I had some apprehension about how I would react when holding the baby and what emotions might overwhelm me. Would I remember the hurt, the resentment of the past? Would the pain return?
When I held her in my arms and looked at the innocent little face, how could I not love her? Slanted eyes, a button of a nose, lots of black hair, cute lips that occasionally smiled. She was a bit restless, disturbed by the change in her routine. When I rocked her she quieted down and rested her little head on my chest. I know she could hear my heart and feel my love

for her. Efelia seemed relaxed. She must be relieved that all is turning out for the best.

When the baby was three or four-months old, Jean-Paul asked if we could invite Efelia and Sabrina to our apartment for a weekend. We had four bedrooms and three bathrooms, so it wasn't as if we didn't have enough space for them.

The challenge I faced was to have them in the privacy of our home. But Jean-Paul wanted to enjoy his baby as much as possible and I reassured myself that although the arrangement was uncomfortable for me, I would learn to live with it. After all, we were in Venezuela for only a few short months. We'd soon be going back to Texas and we'd be away from this constant and at times painful reminder. I was attempting to befriend Efelia because I knew how much it would please my husband.

In the intimacy of our home, I discovered a few truths about her.

When we came back from the pool one day, she didn't bother to dress and remained in her bikini, even as she nursed the baby in our living room. I am all for breastfeeding, having enjoyed doing it myself with our three daughters. It was however quite unsettling to watch how she would expose herself in front of both of us. She was after all my husband's ex-lover. She should show more decency. I spoke to Jean-Paul in French.

"Darling, don't you find your friend somewhat under dressed?"

"Yes, so why don't you say something to her?"

"But she's your friend, my dear. She'd take it better if it came from you."

After their second visit, I knew I could no longer tolerate having them stay with us in our apartment. It no longer mattered how often Jean-Paul would remind me that we could do what others couldn't, that we were this unique couple, with better skills than most other couples at handling such circumstances.

I demanded that Efelia and her baby stay at the Punta Palma Hotel down the road from where we lived, when he flew them from Caracas on subsequent weekends. I had not appreciated the fact that she had offered absolutely no help around the kitchen when I prepared dinner for the three of us. She had not even offered to help clean up afterwards. She acted like a *Prima Donna* and one Sunday night, after she had returned to Caracas, I told Jean-Paul the reasons why I would no longer invite her to stay at our place.

"Did you notice how your friend was just sitting there, reading a magazine, while I was preparing dinner? I had to ask her several times for help. She never once volunteered and it almost seemed to bother her when I asked! What's her problem? It's not as if she's used to being served by maids. Yet I felt that she treated me like one."

Jean-Paul remained silent for several moments. When he finally spoke, he surprised me:

"You know, darling, I also noticed how she was behaving. I'm starting to understand why her mother calls her irresponsible. I'm really disappointed in her and I understand why you won't invite her anymore."

"Thank you! Wow, this is the first time you're actually not defending her. I was afraid you might accuse me of lacking compassion again. I'm glad that you see why I can't tolerate this any more! I did try but I can't do it."

From then on, whenever Efelia and the baby visited us in Puerto La Cruz we invited them to our pool and to the restaurant, but they were no longer our guests in our apartment.

◆   ◆   ◆

I confided in Delphine about my suspicions that some evil force might be at work here. She understood these things, having witnessed them when she lived in Haiti and also in the Dominican Republic. She encouraged me to let Jean-Paul know how sick I had gotten right before coming to Venezuela, when I wore the pendant Efelia had given to me. I shared with her my fears that I might have been under a spell. Didn't I accept passively what I now considered somewhat abusive the invasion of my privacy by having mother and child in my home twice? I had been too tolerant! There was a complete lack of willpower to put my foot down and say NO, even though deep inside, I didn't like the arrangement at all. Why was I so powerless?

One weekend, Jean-Paul had traveled to Miami to visit his family. Efelia and I met in Caracas to have a talk. We had gone shopping together. It was soon after we had let her know her behavior in our apartment was not acceptable. That day I noticed how my perception of Efelia was being altered when I was in her presence. I'd start feeling sorry for her and somewhat guilty of the way I had treated her in the past. If she could have such an effect on me, I wondered what it must be like for Jean-Paul when they met.

Unexplainable bouts with cramps also continued to come out of nowhere. After a weekend in Caracas, I wrote this in my journal:

> *I got sick again this weekend. Severe stomach cramps woke me up and I thought I was going to pass out. Drank hot tea and used the heating pad all night long. The pain came and went like a wave. At one point, it was up in my chest and I was suffocating. Jean-Paul found me bent over the sink sobbing. I felt like a poison was in my system which needed to get out. There's this dark shadow of worry. I feel overwhelmed by the pain, incapacitated and so desperate that I lose all common sense and think of curses and magic power and wonder what is destroying me.*

My friend Soraya had heard me too often point out that I feared I was being attacked. An unknown force seemed to be slowly eating up at my self worth, my customary high level of energy and my spirit. She introduced me to an American Christian minister, Deborah, who came to my home to do a purifying ritual of both the apartment and myself. I started coughing and spitting in an unexpected way during the process, which Deborah explained was a common reaction. It was a deep cough, and the cleansing went on for quite a long time. Deborah used blessed water, blessed oil, said several prayers and recommended that I get rid of everything Efelia had given either Jean-Paul or me. It was true that it irritated me when my husband would wear a particular shirt Efelia had given to him. I knew it was only a shirt, but it provoked such a bad gut feeling that I threw the shirt away, along with every present she had given to us. Deborah wanted to see the bedroom where Efelia and Sabrina had slept. She said some special prayers there and used extra holy water, even under the bed, and inside the armoire. She also made small crosses above the doorframes in all the rooms of the apartment. After Deborah left, I slept soundly for several hours, right in the middle of a sunny afternoon.

Both Delphine and Soraya had given me the same advice about disposing of the gifts from Efelia. Even Belinda Cruz, the Venezuelan acupuncturist I had visited because of a pinched nerve in my neck had told me not to keep anything that came from Efelia in my home. I had not given much attention to their advice up to then. Now that Deborah was also suggesting it, I had no qualms following that recommendation. I knew I'd have some explaining to do when Jean-Paul would be looking for Efelia's presents to him, and I would tell him the truth. The gold charm with the poisonous diamonds went to the bottom of the ocean, the leather wallet she'd bought for him was torn into pieces and thrown in the garbage, as were most of her presents to us ... Had we owned a furnace, that's where everything would have gone. I wanted to burn everything she'd given to us.

The rest of our stay in Venezuela was uneventful. I had gotten over my fears. I no longer experienced sudden attacks of unexplained illnesses. They miraculously disappeared.

◆　　　◆　　　◆

What had started as a three to four months stay in Venezuela had stretched to over a year. Right before Sabrina's birthday, Jean-Paul announced to me that it was time to return home to Houston. I was thrilled to close the book on this chapter of our lives.

In November of that same year, Jean-Paul asked me if we could invite Efelia and Sabrina to join us during our vacation in Costa Rica for three or four days. Why did he want to see them again so soon? Had he not said to me that he would like to see his daughter maybe once a year? This was barely six months since we'd left Venezuela …

Although it was difficult for me to acquiesce, I imagined how it would feel if the roles had been reversed. Had it been my baby, living with her dad, I would be grateful if Jean-Paul allowed me to see her more often than once a year. How could I deny him the pleasure of seeing his young daughter? When he suggested that we could have mother and baby stay with us in our condominium, however, I strongly objected.

The thoughts that raced through my mind were not very positive:

"What is that: a *ménage-à-trois*?" (a threesome) I managed to ask Jean-Paul.

How could we all go on a vacation together? How could he demand this of me? Will the child be calling him *Papa* and her *Mamá*? And where will that leave me? Will I be the *abuela*? (grandmother) Here I was, my reproductive power dwindling, and she would be showing her motherhood in full bloom! I didn't think I could stand it.

I told Jean-Paul he should find them a separate hotel room. I used my positive affirmations:

"Think of peace, of generosity, of love, of forgiveness. Think of how happy Jean-Paul will be. Think of the rewards for showing compassion and kindness to "the poor girl" as he still referred to her. Nobody will know us there. So who cares if someone realized that we were this couple vacationing with an ex-lover and the baby who was born of their affair? Swallow your pride, open your heart, and show more humility. Yield to your husband's desires. Besides, people might think we're the grandparents. Anyway, why should I give importance to what complete strangers might think or say about us?"

There was some deep buried resentment at the thought that I should welcome his ex-lover and their baby in the privacy of our hotel suite. Even though I seemed to accept the arrangement, deep inside, I was not at peace. Wasn't she benefiting from our lifestyle and enjoying a free vacation herself? What right did she have to it?

However, I agreed that four days would be tolerable. So Efelia and Sabrina joined us in Puntarenas, at the Mega-resort Caribbean Village Fiesta Hotel.

The condo our International Resort association had reserved in Costa Rica was an hour away from the capital city of San Jose. We were both happily surprised to see how much privacy our two-bedroom unit would offer us. It was crucial to my peace of mind. I wanted to please my husband but not at the expense of my happiness. Our unit was in the older part of the resort but it was bright and spacious, with two bedrooms and two bathrooms so mother and daughter would have their private quarters.

I kept my focus on what I wanted: harmony and serenity. It all went quite well. Sabrina, who was only 18-months old, loved to "swim". She could stay in the water for hours. And Jean-Paul was never too tired to play with her while I sat in the shade engrossed in John Irving's *A prayer for Owen Meany*.

Efelia would sometimes be in the water with Jean-Paul and Sabrina. Or she'd sit in the shade next to me. We didn't have much to talk about. Our individual lifestyles were poles apart and I certainly didn't feel like engaging in a compatibility contest with her. We did however participate in some poolside activities organized by the resort, including a hoola-hoop contest, which I won, and we also danced in our bikinis to the sound of the Latino music playing for our enjoyment. In the meantime, Jean-Paul watched a napping Sabrina under an umbrella. We lounged by the pool most of the time, ate fresh seafood, drank cold *cervezas* and thanked God that we could all get along so well. *Pura vida* as the Costa Ricans like to say. What a good life!

In the evenings, we were treated to nightly performances put together by the Caribbean Village. One evening was a Michael Jackson impersonation that left us in awe! These four days turned out to be a fun time for all of us. Efelia remembered to cover herself when nursing Sabrina inside the apartment. Jean-Paul noticed that she was not as tactful when we were at an outdoor evening show. When he mentioned to her that she could be more discreet, she shrugged her shoulders and ignored him. I told him it must be due to the way she was brought up.

We had both noticed that little Sabrina wore a red string on her left wrist and left ankle. The mother said it was "for protection".

"This looks like some superstitious custom that my daughter doesn't need," Jean-Paul blurted out one day. He always spoke with Efelia in Spanish, unless he wanted to exchange something with me in private.

"But in my country, it is used to protect small children," she protested.

"Since when do you believe in these stupidities?"

"Since always! And they're not stupidities."

"Do you mean to say that you think these are magic strings?"

"They protect children from illnesses ..."

"This is incredible!"

I let them have their exchange without saying one word. Hadn't Jean-Paul asked her once in front of me if she believed in magic and she had answered negatively? Here she was admitting it candidly.

Jean-Paul asked me in French to find him a pair of scissors or a sharp knife. When I had located a knife in the kitchen, he went into our bedroom with Sabrina, shutting the door behind him and leaving Efelia in the living room with me. I got up to fix us lunch, and didn't look at her. She sat quietly in the living area and didn't say anything when Jean-Paul came out of the room with the red strings removed. Her face was expressionless, although we both knew she was not pleased with what Jean-Paul had just done.

◆   ◆   ◆

We had been back in Houston for a little over a year when Jean-Paul told me of his desire to visit Sabrina before we moved to Europe. We were being transferred to France for a couple of years and Jean-Paul invited me to come along with him to Caracas for a few days before our move. I declined. I didn't like the fact that the political situation at the time was such that the American government had asked all U.S. citizens to evacuate Venezuela. I understood that he wanted to see his daughter. Jean-Paul would have to go there alone. I silently prayed that I wouldn't live to regret my decision. I was thrilled at the idea of moving to Paris, my favorite city in the world. I told Jean-Paul that this was to make up for all the hurt of the past couple of years!

12

The seduction

At the age of 52, I considered myself settled in a satisfying relationship with my husband. On the home front, things were as good as they could be. Jean-Paul traveled occasionally to Indonesia, Malaysia or Venezuela for his job. I had learned to live with the existence of his little girl, a reminder of what had taken place four years ago.

While living in Paris, Jean-Paul had to go to Venezuela for work on two or three occasions. That was an opportunity for him to see Sabrina. There were moments when I felt left out of their little circle when he, Efelia, her son Sergio and Sabrina all got together in Caracas. They must have looked like a complete family. Where did that leave me? However, I knew that there was no longer any attraction on his part towards Efelia. I could trust my husband. He had reassured me convincingly enough. Our relationship had not only survived the affair, but also we had actually grown closer together as a result. I thought that I had the best, and that the rest didn't matter.

Paris was suffering its hottest summer ever. We had been living there for almost a year thanks to the assignment with Jean-Paul's company. It was a dream life. The location of our spacious apartment in the 16th Arrondissement allowed us to explore the city by walking to its most famous landmarks regularly. *La Tour Eiffel, la Seine, les Champs Elysées, l'Arc de Triomphe* and *le Bois de Boulogne* were all within a short walking distance from the *Rue de Longchamp* where we lived.

From the Tour we would walk to the *Place de l'Etoile* and stroll along the Champs Elysées and it became our Friday evening ritual. We would first stop at the *Place du Trocadero* to admire the blinking lights of the most visited monument in the world. The show took place every hour, on the hour, from 19:00 hours until midnight and lasted ten minutes. The tower already impressive during the day took another dimension and we never grew tired of this spectacle. It reminded me of Christmas at Rockefeller Center when they lit the giant tree. Fairytale-like. We thoroughly enjoyed discovering the city's indisputable magnificence. What an amazing gift that was!

On weekends, Jean-Paul and I often traveled both within and outside of France, discovering the very diversified *régions* of the country: *l'Alsace, la Normandie, la Bourgogne, la Loire, la Côte d'Azur*, as well as its neighboring countries Belgium and Germany. We also flew to Portugal, Spain, Italy, Holland and Greece on several occasions. There was so much to do, so many places to visit, we had a busy calendar and my agenda did not include any romance outside of my marriage. I was certainly not dreaming of any involvement with young foreign Romeos. Little did I realize what was about to happen.

What woman, married or single, has not at some point imagined what it would be like to have a French or Italian lover? The movies, magazine articles, books and television shows have helped many fantasize about these European Casanovas and I was no exception.

For the longest time "he" had been a wild dream, an illusion, a reverie. And when I had stopped fantasizing about him, when I had convinced myself that "he" probably would never come along, he just appeared out of nowhere and changed my life unexpectedly. When I first noticed the tall, Italian-looking man at a bus stop near the *Hotel George V*, I may have been smiling. I am the happy kind. Maybe I was humming too. Did that encourage him?

When he searched his pockets for the bus fare, after most riders had already found their seats, I remember thinking to myself:

"Why is he so unprepared? He must not take the bus too often."

I had not realized at this point that I was the only reason he was on that bus.

At the Trocadero stop, he didn't try to hide. He was right behind me, when I crossed the *Avenue d'Eylau* that led to my apartment. I spoke first:

"*Ah, c'est vous! Vous habitez mon quartier?*" (Oh, it's you! Do you live in my neighborhood?")

"*Non, pas du tout.* (No, not at all). I am simply following you!"

"You've got to be kidding! Or is it a habit of yours to follow a woman who is alone in the streets of Paris?"

"No, no. I've not done this before."

Surprised, amused and a bit flattered, I smiled to the stranger he still was to me.

"I'm sorry, but this doesn't happen to me very often and it's hard for me to believe you!"

"It must have happened to you before. You are a very attractive woman. That is why I followed you!"

"Well, you can follow me all you want, but you will have to go back to wherever you came from pretty soon!"

"Why? I thought we could get to know one another." He was persistent.

"And what makes you think I might be interested in this proposition?"

"You smiled to me at the bus stop."

"What? I did not!"

"You wore your sunglasses, I couldn't be sure, but I thought you were looking in my direction a few times."

"Are you serious? I barely noticed you!" I wanted him to know the truth.

"I still would like to get to know you."

"You don't expect me to invite you to my apartment, do you? I don't know you at all!" My reply should have discouraged him.

"My name is Pierre-Alexandre Marais. *Enchanté*." (Pleased to meet you.)

He held out his hand. It was a strong handshake.

I introduced myself as Milena, not wanting him to know my familiar nickname. He said his friends called him Pierre-Alex. His wedding band reassured me that maybe he just wanted to be friendly.

I began to study him. I found him intriguing. He appeared very relaxed in his jeans and button-down white shirt. He wore no socks with his moccasins. He was what the French call *BCBG—Beau Chic, Bon Genre*—well dressed and well bred. I could tell he was *bien dans sa peau* (feeling good in his own skin). His approach captivated me. I kept thinking: "So that's how they operate." I was on my guard. I'd been warned many times about Frenchmen and their reputation. There had been a few instances when I had noticed men following me, but they were in their car, and it had been easy to get rid of them. I'd just walk up or down a one-way street they couldn't access, and it would be the end of the pursuit. Or if a man asked me to join him for a drink, I'd smile and decline, thank him and keep on walking. It was part of the French culture. I knew it was typical for Frenchmen to pay that kind of a compliment to women. Why was I paying so much attention to this one? Was I going to play along?

Initially, I did all I could to discourage him:

"I am a very happily married woman and I'm really not looking for any adventure. You are wasting your time."

I said it with a smile. He smiled back and kept on walking right behind me. I went into the health store around the corner from my apartment building to pick up a few items. He followed me inside, where we both welcomed the conditioned air. We made small talk. I was wondering how I would get rid of this persistent young man.

When we reached my building, I turned to him and extended my hand for a final handshake: "Let's just say *au revoir*. This is where I live, and you must go now."

"You are not inviting me for a drink? It is so hot today!"

It was probably close to 40 degrees centigrade! (104 degrees Fahrenheit) I hesitated and shook my head in disbelief. I knew it was unbearably hot and I was somewhat dehydrated. I didn't want to seem to encourage him in any way though.

"Just one little glass, you can trust me. I will behave, you have nothing to fear."

He reassured me by saying: "I will be a gentleman."

I looked into his eyes. I evaluated him and thought silently: "I'm a big girl. I can defend myself. He doesn't look too threatening."

I yielded: "If I do invite you in, let's make one thing clear: it won't be for wine or any kind of liquor, and you promise to behave yourself."

We remained formal all afternoon long. Pierre-Alex was courteous. I was curious. We listened to the CDs I had just purchased and I confessed that music was one of my passions. A couple of hours had gone by when he asked me what I thought of our encounter. I admitted being a bit puzzled. We had shared a few life experiences with one another. I had enjoyed his conversation very much. Now I wanted a few details:

"When exactly did you decide to follow me?"

"At the Virgin Records store."

"Really? I never noticed you until the bus stop."

"Non, non, I saw you at Virgin, upstairs. You picked all these disks. Then you were about to leave the store, you noticed another one and you went back to the register to pay for it. *On est d'accord?*" (We agree?)

"You were watching me the whole time?"

"Yes, and you were completely oblivious!"

"And when I started walking towards my home? Were you behind me?

"Yes, of course!"

"You got on the bus not even knowing where I was going?"

"I was following you."

"You're a dangerous man."

"Not at all, *au contraire*. I'm very gentle."

"Frankly, I'm intrigued. This seems like a novel or a movie."

"How do you think it will end?"

"I have not the faintest idea. I think we'll just say goodbye and move on with our lives. We are both married, and as I have told you before, I'm in a very good relationship, and not looking for any adventure!"

I was secretly thinking: "Man follows woman in the streets of Paris and makes passionate love to her in her 16th arrondissement apartment." What a story! But I could not tell any of my girlfriends about it. What would they think?

I reassured myself that this would not happen by telling Pierre-Alex one more time: "I'm in love with my husband and we've been happily married for 30 years!"

He flattered me: "*On vous a cueilli au berceau!*" (You were taken from the cradle!) "You look too young to have been married this long!"

I asked him how old he was. 34. I told him my age before he inquired. He said I looked like I was *dans la trentaine* (in my 30's). Even though I had heard this kind of remark before, he was endearing himself to my heart with his compliment. I couldn't help smiling: not only did we have the same difference in age as Jean-Paul and Efelia, but we were exactly of the same age as they were when they had become lovers! Wouldn't it be interesting if …?

My new friend was very self-assured. He suggested boldly that we could make love all afternoon long and that it would be a great way to spend our time together. There was something fascinating in his approach. I didn't let him know how my line of thinking had paralleled his.

"That is absolutely out of the question. I'll have to ask you to leave." I assured him.

"*Non, non, non, je vous en supplie* (No, no, no, I implore you). We can just continue to talk."

"Please. You promised you would behave." I reminded him.

"I am. Can I sit next to you on the couch?"

I let him. When he did, we both started laughing: there was a kitchen knife on the cocktail table. I had used it to open my new cd's. It was staring at us.

"It's to defend myself in case you try anything silly!" I said smiling.

Pierre-Alex delicately brushed my neck and bare shoulders with his fingers, slowly, very gently. I felt vulnerable, a weakness of mine. I asked him to stop and he complied. I admitted to myself that I had enjoyed his touch and I almost wished I had not stopped him. At that moment I began to see a possibility: what if we met again? Could that dream of long ago be rekindled? Pierre-Alex had languorous hazel eyes, a small mouth, his straight black hair was neatly combed back and a deep cleft marked his chin. He was 6 feet tall, quite attractive, well built, had nice hands and lots of hair on his chest and arms. He carried an intelligent conversation, said he liked to read and enjoyed poetry. I caught myself imagining what it would be like to be seduced by him.

"Out of the question," I reassured myself silently. "Why would I want to have an affair at this stage of my life? He is a complete stranger."

And that's exactly what made it exciting: he was a stranger and no one needed to know. I would tell Jean-Paul one day, after we had left France.

It would not happen today though, of that I was certain. I needed at least the weekend to think about it. I needed to get to know him better.

I got up from the couch: "I've enjoyed the afternoon. I thank you for behaving, and let's just say goodbye."

He smiled a beautiful smile, kissed me on the cheek, touched my lips with his fingers and left after jotting down my telephone number. I asked him for his, perhaps so I'd have some proof that I had not imagined the entire episode.

He said he would call on Monday. When he left, I felt nostalgic. It was a weekend that I would be spending alone because Jean-Paul was in Malaysia on a business trip and Suzanna and Danielle had just gone back home after spending a couple of weeks with us in the South of France.

I could not stop thinking about my new friend all weekend long, and I wondered if he would call. Why would he, when he must have gotten the message that I was not interested in getting involved in any kind of romantic affair? But on the following Monday, he asked if I could join him for a *petit café*. I declined. That was crazy!

"How about tomorrow? Do you want to have lunch with me?"

"No, I won't be available for lunch."

"A drink then? After lunch? *Un petit jus de citron.* You pick the place."

"OK, there's an outdoor café at Trocadero. Café Carette. I'll be there at two." I had decided I should at least meet him one more time.

When I saw him smoking a cigarette, having his *petit café* at our rendez-vous spot, near the Trocadero *Metro*, I foolishly desired that he would become my lover. I had spent the weekend fantasizing about what it would be like. I found him quite *séduisant* (appealing), dressed in business attire: a crisp gray shirt, blue and gray striped tie, dark gray pants and elegant Italian leather shoes.

He got up to pull the chair for me. I asked him to put his cigarette out and he complied, after first arguing that we were outdoors and that the smoke should not bother me.

I ordered a *menthe à l'eau*. It was refreshing on another very hot summer day.

When our eyes met, I saw a question in his. When I looked away, he already possessed me. He touched my hand, my naked arm, my bare shoulder and I shivered despite the intense heat. In that moment we dropped the use of the '*vous*' form of you we had been using up to then, and switched to the '*tu*' form. That came naturally to both of us.

We spoke for a while. He asked how I felt.

"Obviously, if I'm meeting with you, I must be a bit mad! Or maybe this intense heat is giving me a high fever!" We both laughed.

I kept shaking my head, refusing to believe that I was really considering this liaison. Pierre Alex suggested that we go to my place once we had finished our drinks. He drove us there although it was only a couple of blocks away.

I knew the concierge was watching everyone who entered the building. So when we walked toward the elevator, I acted as if we weren't together. What if our neighbors saw us? Mind you, it was not as if we were friends with any of them. But I still felt uncomfortable. What was I doing? Was I out of my mind? Did I not fear the consequences?

When we got inside, we had some chilled Brouilly, a light red wine now a favorite since I had found out it could be served cold. I put some music on: Norah Jones, Buddha Bar, Sidney Bechet; the same artists we had listened to on Friday. He recognized some of the tunes.

I was slightly nervous. Here I was with a handsome young man in my living room. I knew he wanted to have sex with me. It felt completely natural, and at the same time quite strange. We barely knew one another. What was he doing in my apartment?

I started to panic and told him that maybe he should leave. He just smiled and said nothing would happen until I was ready.

"Pierre-Alex, you're going to need to be very patient with me. We don't have to become lovers so quickly."

He reassured me: "*Je suis un amant très doux*" (I'm a very gentle lover).

The way he said it made me believe him. He indulged me in a very long foot and calf massage that delighted and relaxed me.

"I want you to understand one thing: I don't want to fall in love. I'm already in love with my husband."

"Who is talking about falling in love? We're just going to be lovers. That's all."

"Ah? I guess I'll let you show me what it's like to 'just be lovers!'"

"Just relax. Today is only for you. You're not yet ready for me."

I thanked him for being so attentive to my needs. He had guessed that I was troubled and he held me in a comforting embrace before we parted. I noticed my lipstick all over his collar and asked him to remove his shirt so I could wash and iron it for him. He took a shower while I got rid of the evidence. The whole thing felt like a dream from which I would soon wake.

As he left, I watched from our balcony overlooking the street. He threw me a kiss before starting his car and driving away.

Oh my! What have I done? I was having an affair! What was my husband going to say when I told him about it? I knew he would understand. But why should I tell him now if it was going to cause undue upset? I would wait until we had left France. And what if Pierre-Alex never called again?

We would take it one step at a time. I was surprised to feel as little guilt as I did. I needed to ask myself one question: would I have allowed Pierre-Alex to become my lover if Jean-Paul hadn't been unfaithful? Not that it justified what I had done in any way. It simply helped me to understand how easily one can be seduced, when the barrier of resistance is let down. There was perhaps a part of me that wanted to get even. It may not have been on the conscious level, but it was there, and thinking about what had just happened made me smile. When I confided in Pierre-Alex about how I felt, he asked me:

"Are you planning to tell your husband so you can get your revenge?"

"Not right away, no, but he will know, believe me. I will probably tell him when we leave Paris."

One thing I didn't want was for my feelings to get in the way. I was not going to allow myself to become sentimentally attached to Pierre-Alex. I needed to keep the relationship strictly on a physical level. We would only be in Paris for a short while and I certainly didn't want to fall in love now and risk another heartbreak when having to say goodbye!

On his way back to his office, he called from his cell phone to find out how I was feeling. I told him that the whole episode seemed like a scene from a movie.

"Is it to be continued?"

"Maybe. Call me next week and we will see!"

13

The liaison (Pierre-Alexandre)

«La faim et l'amour sont les deux axes du monde. L'humanité roule toute entière sur l'amour et la faim » (Hunger and love are the two pivots that make the world go round. Mankind revolves entirely around love and hunger.)

Anatole France wrote this to George Sand and I agree with him. For me, making love or giving love to a woman is as important as eating.

I have a new *amante*. She looks exotic, and when I first saw her I thought she was from South America, Brazil perhaps. She is an island girl. Yes, I can see that now. The way she swings her hips when she walks, the way she arks her back and squares her shoulders, and of course it's in her accent, even in her native French. She is a Créole.

She holds her chin up and her back very straight. She has the allure of a dancer. There is an attitude of pride due to her belief that her ancestors came from royalty: she told me that on her father's side there was a Polish princess, and also a Baron. She had a Jamaican grandmother with a stiff British upbringing that dictated strict rules: "Children should be seen, not heard." The grandmother had insisted that the children sit on their hands. This way they could not gesticulate when they spoke. This did not work too well because she uses her hands as much as the Italians to indicate her opinion of things.

She has inherited her table manners from her grandparents and her parents, and when she sets the table for our lunchtime rendezvous, she uses her good silver, nice crystal glasses and her Limoges china. I pointed out to her that she must have been brought up *à la Française*. She uses cloth napkins and decorates the table with fresh flowers and candles. When I made the comment that she had good taste, she looked surprised that I paid attention to every detail. I also observe the way she dresses, very *bourgeois*, or when she combs her hair a different way, or how she decorates her apartment.

She is elegant and sophisticated. Her level of energy rivals that of younger women. She says it's because she's a vegetarian who only on occasion eats fish. She seldom indulges in the rich food we Frenchmen love so much. She does not drink coffee either but she knows how to prepare it strong, just the way I like it. Sometimes I tease her that she is doing *carême* (observing Lent) all year long.

She is always happy when I call to tell her I am coming for a visit. Actually, she is always happy. She claims to be the happiest person she knows, and I see why it is so.

She loves to surprise me when I visit. When she opens the door I never know if she will be in a Japanese kimono and call herself my Geisha, or in a Hawaiian muumuu with flowers in her hair or around her neck, saying Aloha, or in a tight, silk Chinese dress, slit on both sides. Once she has worn a daring black outfit, her black high-heels leather boots, and a Carnival mask from New Orleans. I told her laughingly that all she needed was the whip! She said she had been inspired by something she read in a book on romance. I like that she is so carefree and *très à l'aise* (very comfortable) in her new role as my *maîtresse*. That is what I call her when she calls me *"mon amant"* (my lover).

She wears her hair a different way each time I see her: curly one day, straight the next time. She lets it down or pulls it in a bun like a Spanish dancer. She highlights it red, purple, burgundy or copper. She is many women in one. She is fun to be with, playful and entertaining too. She says that I am too quiet and she has invited me many times to confide in her.

She has opened herself to me, without any pretense, and I like that she can be so authentic.

She wanted to know how a younger man like me could find pleasure in the company of a woman her age. Her self-confidence was one of the first things that captivated me. I find that very sexy in a woman. She's very self-assured. It is apparent in the way she carries herself, in the way she makes eye contact. She is very direct, very assertive. She also has a conversation that is more intellectual than that of younger women. If there is a reason for everything that happens in life, then I am in hers to bring her pleasure. For a short time maybe, but I knew from the first time we met that it would be passionate. She wanted to find some kind of meaning to our idyll and I told her to just relax and enjoy it. It was helping her to understand other situations she did not want to talk about. She was becoming less judgmental of women she knew who took lovers and cheated on their husbands. They were adulteresses, and now she was one. They were sleeping with married men, and now she was too. And she admitted feeling only a little bit of shame, and very little remorse.

She often said that she deserved to have all the pleasure I was giving her. She wanted to tell her husband about us but I asked her to wait. Even if he can be understanding and forgiving, even if he will let her continue to see me, as she was so certain of, I preferred not to face that situation.

I asked her once if she thought her husband had ever cheated on her. She looked at me with a sad smile and said: "What do you think? Don't most men cheat on their wives? I would not have gotten involved with you if he had not been unfaithful."

"How did you find out?"

"He told me himself."

"You're joking, right? I certainly would never tell my wife!"

"Well, you don't have the kind of friendship with your wife that my husband and I share."

She didn't like to talk about it but she had suffered a big disappointment a few years before, and it was still hurtful to speak about it.

"The only reason why I don't tell my husband about us is because it might hurt his pride. I prefer to wait until we are no longer in France, then it will be easier for him to deal with it. It's too painful to find out while your spouse is still involved with another partner."

She came back by asking me: "Have you ever loved two women at the same time with almost the same degree of intensity?"

"No, not really. Is that what happened to your husband?"

"Yes, with his secretary. And now he has a three-year old little girl to remind us both of that situation."

"Is he still involved with the mother?"

"Of course not, you think I'd still be with him? He does visit them every year though."

"Alone?"

"Yes."

I had to ask: "And you don't think that they are still lovers?"

"No, I know they're not. He would tell me. We say everything to each other."

"You haven't told him about us!"

"Not yet. But I will!"

We didn't speak about my relationship with my wife Laurence. The first time we met, Mia had told me that I should go home to my wife and make love to her instead of trying to seduce her. I didn't understand why she even brought my wife into our conversation. I was puzzled and told her that one thing had nothing to do with the other and to leave my wife out of the discussion. She knew I loved my family. We both knew that what we had between us was just an interlude, a way to pass the time. We were both consenting adults enjoying a good time together.

She had told me that they would be relocating to America in a few months, so our encounter was for a short time only. But I wanted to see her as often as I could before she left.

We sometimes recited French poetry. One of our favorites was Verlaine: *Mon rêve familier* (My familiar dream).

Je fais souvent ce rêve étrange et pénétrant
D'une femme inconnue et que j'aime, et qui m'aime,
Et qui n'est, chaque fois, ni tout à fait la même,
Ni tout à fait une autre, et m'aime et me comprend.
Car elle me comprend, et mon coeur transparent
Pour elle seule, hélas! cesse d'être un problème …

(I often dream this strange and penetrating dream
Of an unknown woman whom I love and who loves me,
And who is, each time, not quite the same
Nor yet quite different, and loves and understands me.
For she understands me, and my transparent heart
For her alone, alas, ceases to be a challenge …)

She appreciated the beautiful language that French is. She read a lot in both French and English and I liked to exchange opinions with her about books we had both read. I enjoyed hearing her description of the many places she had visited. The time we spent together was simply not long enough.

On one of my visits to her apartment, I almost bumped into her husband in the lobby. I recognized him from the pictures in their living room.

It was a bit 'risqué' to pay her a visit at such a late hour. My business meetings had lasted longer than I had planned and the lunch she had prepared for us would be their dinner. I had called two times to apologize and, noticing the late hour, I had suggested postponing until the next week since it was a Friday.

But she had begged me to come anyway assuring me that her husband would not be home until after 18:00 hours. It was just past 17:30 hours when I was ready to leave. She wouldn't let me go, though. I joked that if the doorbell rang and the front door opened, I might have to jump in my Adam's suit from her second floor balcony, run into the clothing store downstairs and ask the salesladies to dress me from head to toes so that I could walk down the street to my car! That made her laugh *aux éclats* (out loud).

In the end we came close to being caught by him. But she didn't fear his reaction at all. She thought he'd be very cordial and would shake my hand and say: "So you're my wife's lover?"

I couldn't be so sure what kind of reaction he would have, so I hurried out and took the stairway instead of the elevator. As I was opening the door leading to the *rez-de-chaussée* (lobby), I saw him conversing with the concierge right in front of the elevator.

When I later told her that she had taken a big chance, she shrugged her shoulders and laughed: "Maybe that's what I secretly desire: to be caught *en flagrant délit*" (red-handed).

«*Le coeur a ses raisons que la raison ne connaît pas*» (The heart has its own reasons that reason itself does not understand)! I often told Mia it was especially true of the heart of women and hers was no exception!

14

Suspicions (Jean-Paul)

My wife asked me a strange question completely out of the blue:

"Darling, I have a hypothetical question for you: if I ever got involved with another man, would you prefer to know while it's happening or when it's all over?"

"Do you have something you want to tell me?"

Mia continued:

"I just wonder if you're like me, wanting to know everything right away, or if you'd prefer not to be aware of anything if I ever started seeing someone else."

"You know me ... I'd like to know when you are ready to tell me."

"If you came home one day and didn't find me, what would you do?"

What was Mia alluding to? Had she met someone?

"I'd go visit your friend Rachelle and ask her where you were." I replied, still wondering what she wasn't telling me.

"What if you came home and found me with another man?"

"I'd probably go see Rachelle and seek comfort in her arms." Rachelle worked in a boutique two or three doors down from our apartment.

"You're always joking! Tell me really, how would you feel?"

"I'd be happy for you! And it excites me just to think about it!" I was downplaying the apprehension Mia's questions were triggering. I wanted her to confide in me if she had something to share. I said it jokingly, and deep inside, I was shaken. Was my wife just teasing me or was she really considering leaving me for another man? She would not have spoken so candidly, I reassured myself.

I attempted to recall what could have led me to suspect that she may have met someone. There was a particular Friday evening, when I returned home after a short trip out of town, when she took me by surprise and asked me to make love to her right there on our living room couch! She had lowered the blinds and lit some candles and the place looked quite different. I had wondered then if Mia was playing the role of seductress. There was suddenly some apprehension on my part. Yet I didn't want to interrogate her. She would tell me if there was anything to tell.

Now I was remembering how she had wanted to try something different in bed on a couple of occasions.

She always welcomed me with such a radiant smile when I arrived home in the evening, and she was always eager when I wanted to make love to her. I shouldn't feel jealous of this stranger. I should have prepared myself for this eventuality. Europeans in general didn't regard infidelity in the same manner as North Americans did. In that sense I was more European than American. Mia had shared with me what some of her Parisian friends considered natural. An encounter between lovers in the afternoon was not so unusual. They talked about it with the same ease they'd talk about having a cup of tea. It was part of their heritage.

I did not ask her for the name of her lover. I couldn't be sure that he truly existed. She would tell me when she was ready.

When did I first suspect that there might be someone else? Maybe it was when we were vacationing in the South of Italy: Mia had asked me to retrieve her messages from her portable telephone. There was a male voice on her answering machine and he sounded quite friendly. When I asked her who it was she gave me a vague answer: "A possible client for my coaching services."

Later that day she went out for a walk on the beach and took her cellular phone with her. I'm sure she must have called him back. I didn't probe.

Another time was when we were in the Netherlands with our three girls. Her phone rang and she left the room to speak to her caller. She stayed in the corridor outside our hotel room for several minutes, and when I asked her afterwards who had called, she said it was her friend Marie-Ange and that she needed privacy to discuss a personal issue with her.

Then, right after the New Year, we were all in the kitchen when her cellular phone rang and Mia simply went into our bedroom to take the call, shutting the door behind her. One of our daughters had asked me who was calling and I hadn't known what to reply. She didn't stay on the phone very long, and didn't offer any explanation as to who had been calling. And I didn't want to ask in front of our daughters. There was a certain look on her face, a *je-ne-sais-quoi* (I don't know what) that made me wonder who this mysterious caller was.

Sometimes, I think Mia would be justified if she sought the companionship of another man. Didn't I betray her trust when I strayed? I had hoped that she would not be so deeply affected. But she had suffered a great deal of uncertainty as a result of my behavior. I wondered at times if she knew how much I loved her. I didn't always know how to demonstrate my love for her. And now there was a possibility of a man in her life who was giving her something she was missing from our relationship. Mia often said I was taking her for granted. She complained of being treated like a maid. She was a wonderful homemaker who tastefully decorated our residences. Maybe I didn't pay enough attention to the care she took to make the apartment an elegant home. If he truly existed, how was her lover treating her? Was he showing her more appreciation for her efforts?

At the end of our first year in Paris, I decided to write a list of the things I appreciated in Mia. I gave it to her when she went away to the Bahamas to celebrate her birthday with her friends:

My love,
I've decided to let you know some of the things you are to me:
First and foremost, you are my friend. The one I share so many memories

with, the one that stood by me and understood me during the worst crisis of our marriage, when even some of your best friends were setting you up against me. Your friendship is the most valuable gift that you could have ever given to me.

You are my lover. By far the most passionate and exciting lover I have ever had or could ever dream of. I must be the envy of most men.

You are my wondrous and forgiving wife, who is committed to her vows to stick with me for better or for worse.

You are a wonderful and caring mother. You have raised our three daughters almost single-handedly while I was traveling, and you have helped them become very mature and balanced individuals.

You are the best cook I could ever dream of, and sometimes you surpass even my mother in the kitchen.

You are my homemaker who always makes sure that the house looks impeccable when I come home and always can decorate a home better than a well-respected home designer.

You are my fashion adviser who always makes sure that I look my best when I go out and provides me with up to date outfits when my old clothes look out of style.

You are my motivator when the world is gloomy and I do not trust myself in a difficult situation.

You are my attentive listener when I have a secret to share or when I need to confide in someone.

You are my inspirational teacher who brings home all the spiritual teachings of the masters and puts them to practice.

You are my health and food specialist who will insure my longevity with the right diet and food combination.

You are my spirited and vivacious party maker who can turn any dull gathering into a fun event.

You are my best dance partner who has kept me agile and young on the dance floor.

You are my constant reminder of empowering words.
You are my angel and my conscience when I am on the wrong path.
You are my role model when faced with an intimidating situation.
You are my partner for life, the one who has supported me and is continu-
ing to support me in all my endeavors.
I could probably add a dozen more of the things that you are to me, but it
might go to your head.
I love you and wish you a wonderful birthday in the Bahamas.

I hoped that Mia would keep this list and read it when she started feeling uncertain about my love for her, or, as she had confessed to me, when
she wondered if I could leave her for someone else.

She had become less confident since my involvement with Efelia. She
had seen me in love with someone else for the first time since we'd known
one another. She had been stunned by the revelation. Even though I've
reassured her I no longer feel any attraction towards Efelia, our friendship
disturbs her. How can I help Mia understand that I've become completely
disenchanted with my little girl's mother? It has not been as difficult as I
had imagined to get over my feelings for her. The disappointment caused
by the suspicion that she might have orchestrated the whole pregnancy
episode helped me detach. My feelings for her started changing when Sabrina was an infant. There was further release when I witnessed Mia's tolerance when we vacationed together in Costa Rica. The physical distance
between us when we returned to Texas and moved to be here in Paris also
contributed to the detachment.

One thing I know for sure is that Mia and I are soul mates. A relationship such as ours is not commonly found, and only happens once in a lifetime. This is why I treasure it. That is why I knew that if indeed Mia were
seeing another man, I would show her that I too had the heart to forgive
her infidelity. But what if she were to leave me for him?

15

The admission

A few days after the New Year, Jean-Paul and I traveled to the nearby city of Troyes, where we were to spend the night.

We were listening to Jacques Brel singing: *Mon amour, mon doux, mon tendre, mon merveilleux amour.* (My beloved, my sweet, my gentle, my wonderful love). I appreciated Brel's '*Chanson des vieux amants*' (Old lovers' song) more than ever in that moment. It spoke of the love of a couple after they'd been together for twenty years. It had survived the husband taking off a thousand times (*Mille fois je pris mon envol*), and the wife taking a few lovers to help time go by (*Il fallait bien passer le temps*). It spoke of suitcases packed many times and of reconciliations. We sang with Brel and we sang to each other.

We discussed what had happened to us the previous night. Jean-Paul caressed my hand or stroked my knee to reassure me that everything was going to be fine.

The love I felt for my husband right then was profound. It was full of wonderful memories that far outweighed the times when I suffered because of my inability to let go of my attachment to him. I now believed that in order to truly love, one must be able to set the other one free.

Chloe, Suzanna and Danielle had left after spending the Christmas holidays with us. We had driven to neighboring Belgium and Holland with them. We had also visited the *Palais de Versailles* and our favorite Loire Castle, Chambord. It had been a wonderful family vacation. We were delighted to have all three daughters with us at this time of the year. Chloe had returned to Santa Fe where she now lived. Suzanna flew back to Phoenix and Danielle left for Austin.

On the following Friday evening, we each had already enjoyed several glasses of red wine at dinner and Jean-Paul opened another bottle that he brought to our study with two glasses. He programmed our CD player with several soundtracks and he invited me to sit comfortably on the couch next to him.

When I've had too much to drink, I often start speaking loudly and profusely and I laugh a lot. Jean-Paul has the opposite reaction. He becomes quiet, pensive, lost in his thoughts.

We were both feeling very mellow by the time we finished the wine. I knew that Jean-Paul wanted to speak to me. He had been unusually quiet since the girls' departure. I wasn't sure what was troubling him. I was feeling woozy.

I was singing in Italian, along Bocelli performing on our Bose. Jean-Paul said he had something he wanted to talk about.

"There seem to be two Mias, one very nice, smiling and full of light, and another one who is gray and who often nags. I like the first one much better." He paused. Then: "One of the two Mias has a secret she needs to share."

What was he saying?

"You can tell me what you have to say, you know?" Jean-Paul continued.

"What are you talking about?" I was giggling. I was feeling very light headed. Why was he asking me this now? I wasn't exactly coherent! He repeated:

"I already know, darling. You can tell me."

In my confused state, I thought that he was alluding to a poem I had written in French about Pierre-Alex. There was no name, just a few verses. I had printed it and had forgotten to remove it from the tray. So maybe he had read it and that's why he was probing. I showed him the poem.

"Is this what you're talking about?"

He barely glanced at it.

"Whom is it for?"

"It's something Marie-Ange wrote about a man she's been seeing." I lied. "She asked me to print it for her."

"Darling, I told you that I already know what you have to tell me."

My mind was going in all directions. Why was he bringing this up now? Not when I was so confused and intoxicated. Not when I was losing touch with reality and felt so vulnerable and scattered. If I told him, he might have prevented me from having further contact with Pierre-Alex. I wasn't ready to give up our clandestine rendezvous. What could I do? What should I tell Jean-Paul?

I was biting my lower lip so I wouldn't say anything I might regret. Jean-Paul was smiling lovingly:

"Mia, several weeks ago you asked me if I would want to know while you were having an affair or after it was over. That was a definite clue. I'm really happy for you if you have met someone. It's okay. You can tell me!"

I suppose that, deep inside, one of the reasons we drank so much was to be in an altered state so we could be more open with one another. Jean-Paul had a few things he wanted to say to me. I opened up to him, when I realized how much love he was showing me, how much understanding and total acceptance he had of my current situation. I owed it to the friend I had in my life partner to share my secret with him:

"Are you sure you want to hear more? I'm still seeing him, you know?"

"Are you in love with him?"

"Of course not! I'm fond of him. You know how women are: we just can't be intimate with a man and not become sentimental about it."

Jean-Paul had a few questions.

"Married?"

"Yes, two kids. I should feel horrible, but his wife has no idea and I feel no guilt."

"Who knows about it?"

"Rachelle. Rachelle knows because she's my closest friend in Paris. And I needed to tell someone. I haven't even told Dana and she's my best friend! I want to see her face when I tell her! So it will have to wait until we're back in the States."

"How do you feel toward him?"

"Of course I like him, but I'm not madly in love with him. He has never said *"Je t'aime"* to me. Maybe *"Je suis fou de toi"* (I'm crazy about you). But it is not a very romantic affair. The last thing I want is to fall in love with someone else. And he knows I would never leave you for anyone. It's a first for me to be able to be with another man, a married man, over so many months, with such little shame or guilt. I'm sorry to be so blunt, but that's the truth!"

I kept looking at Jean-Paul in an attempt to detect any signs of upset. He was hiding it well if he felt any.

"I'm taking this one day at a time," I continued, "since I know that we will soon be saying goodbye. Now, I understand you so much more, for having had this experience myself. I'm not trying to justify what I've done in any way, but it happened when I was feeling lonely! And at this stage of my life, I was starting to believe that I was no longer attractive to anyone! So to have this young man show interest in me is flattering. It feels really good to my ego."

Jean-Paul asked what I suppose is customary: Was Pierre-Alex attentive to my needs? Did he treat me well? Was he a good lover?

"He's very good to me, and he knows how to please a woman, and he definitely is not the kind of lover one fantasizes about: no flowers, no gifts, not even chocolates. And that's fine with me. Otherwise, I'd probably let myself fall in love with him and it would be too hard to say goodbye when we go home. I'm very fond of him. Not in love. That's all."

"Well, I'm happy for you."

Once I had shared my secret with him, I wanted to laugh and cry all at the same time. Our emotions were raw, our thoughts were scattered, but one thing became clear to both of us: we truly wanted happiness for one another.

Jean-Paul reassured me that he was not hurt by my confession.

"I should maybe thank your friend for the new person I see emerging in you!"

What an amazing man my husband was. I was relieved that I had confided in him. He suggested that I not let Pierre-Alex know that he was aware of the situation. I had already decided that when I saw him the following week I wouldn't tell my lover about our exchange. It might make him uncomfortable.

The night we spent in the city of Troyes was bittersweet. I knew my confession had saddened my husband. I had noticed tears in his eyes in the car, on the way from Paris to Troyes, as we reminisced the previous night. He didn't say much. But I knew what it felt like to find out that your spouse had strayed, especially if it is an ongoing situation. I could guess what emotions Jean-Paul was going through. It doesn't matter how insignificant straying may appear to some, finding out that your spouse has been with another partner hurts. The person betrayed goes through an array of emotions. Pain, uncertainty, insecurity, deception, sadness, despair, doubt or hatred are experienced at different levels. I had gone through these emotions. Jean-Paul was now experiencing what I had dealt with for quite some time. Deep inside of me, there was a slightly pleasing thought that maybe he now would know how damaging it is for a spouse to go through the trauma of betrayal. It was a bittersweet revenge!

16

Resolutions
(Jean-Paul)

Mia went back to Paris to say goodbye to her friend. When she told me that she wanted to attend a course on travel reporting in Paris, I immediately understood that she needed a reason to go back to France alone. She was often melancholy when she thought about him. I could see it in her eyes. And I remembered the tears when we left Paris. She had been greatly disappointed the day before we were leaving, because he had been unable to meet her for their last goodbyes. On the morning of departure, she told me she had a bad ear infection and would not be able to fly. I reassured her that she'd be fine. I was certainly not going to leave my wife alone in Paris.

That is why she now wanted the opportunity to say goodbye. I would not prevent her from going. It had been four months since we had left France to return to Texas. Mia had been invited to be the featured speaker at a meeting of an International Women's group in Paris. Since that coincided with her plans to attend the writing course, she eagerly made her travel arrangements. She was thrilled at the opportunity to share with an audience why she claims to be the happiest woman she knows. Her passion for public speaking hasn't diminished and she will no doubt share with them many inspiring stories. I am always awed by the ease with which my wife can share personal details of her life with complete strangers. Is she looking for sympathy from them when she opens herself and exposes details of our lives I'd rather keep private?

Her trip was coinciding with Sabrina's fourth birthday. As soon as I mentioned to her my plans to visit Sabrina for her birthday, Mia had brought up the fact that she wanted to go back to Paris. I wished for her to have fun in Europe.

I know she was grateful that I let her return to Paris so she could say *adieu* to her Frenchman. It may have been the last time they saw one another. She must realize how difficult it is to keep this long distance romance. I knew she had grown fond of him. That was almost inevitable.

When Mia returned home from Paris, she had to come to terms with the fact that her affair would be ending naturally. They were separated by a vast ocean. The distance surely made the relationship a challenge.

I let her know right away that when I was in Venezuela, I had invited Efelia, her son Sergio and Sabrina to spend the night in my hotel room in. Caracas. I had decided that if I wanted to have my daughter for the night, the only way it would happen was to also have the mother and the brother stay with me. Sabrina was extremely shy and had a strong attachment to her mother. She would not accept to stay alone with me. The four of us had an innocent sleepover at the Embassy Suite Hotel. My wife did not see it as such.

"What were you thinking about? How did you think I would react to this arrangement?"

"It was just a pajama party!"

"Why do you do these things you know are going to upset me? Do you want me to leave you? You are so irresponsible! This is the *coup de grâce* (fatal blow) to our relationship. Did you think I would just smile and say nothing? And how could Efelia show such a lack of decency? This shows a complete lack of respect for my feelings from both of you."

"I don't see why you make such a big deal of this," I replied. "You know how I feel about Efelia. We're just friends. And both kids were there with us!"

"I don't care if her mother was there as well. This is not acceptable. This is a woman who has been your lover. Her son is old enough to understand a few things and that is setting such a wrong example for both kids."

"What do you mean? The mother ended up sleeping with her daughter in one bed and Sergio slept in my bed because Sabrina wouldn't sleep with me. That was an innocent arrangement."

I thought that by now Mia knew with enough confidence that there was no longer any physical attraction on my part towards Efelia. What we have between us is a deep friendship but it was hard for my wife to accept the level of intimacy she thought we still maintained.

"That was quite disrespectful towards me, if you want to know! How could you think I would not be upset!?"

I was speechless. Why was Mia overreacting? Had she become so insecure that she couldn't understand that all I wanted was to be closer to my daughter? Besides, hadn't she just been with her lover in Paris? I didn't want to allude to it. I already knew what she would say: "It wasn't the same thing!"

The fact that I was on company's business, and that I had almost been seen by a colleague with both kids and their mother entering my hotel room infuriated my wife. She asked if I didn't care to be caught in such compromising situation.

Of course I would prefer that no one I knew saw me with them. And I also understood that Mia's Frenchman would always remain a stranger to me, whereas Efelia was going to be in our lives because she is my daughter's mother. It made it more difficult for my wife to accept our ongoing friendship.

Mia decided:

"You know what I'll do: I will e-mail your friend to let her know what I think of this kind of behavior so she knows that if you should ever invite her again, she should have the good sense to decline. I want you to review the letter before I send it."

There had been past incidents when Efelia had complained to me about what Mia had said or written. This time, I read the letter before she sent it and gave my approval.

The reply from Efelia was quite arrogant as she blatantly stated that Mia surely wanted to prevent me from seeing my daughter and that my wife was jealous of the little girl. She told Mia that she should not waste her time with such stupidities. My wife was furious. There was such venom in Efelia's letter that Mia decided that she had simply gone too far and that she would completely ignore her. When I discussed the exchange of mail with Efelia on the telephone, I insisted that she send an apology but this incident prompted Mia to comment that she would have no further contact with Sabrina's mother.

"What gives her the right to address me in this manner? Who does she think she is? Ah non, non, non! I want nothing to do with her. This girl has some nerve!"

She paused briefly. Then:

"Did you by any chance say anything to her about my relationship with Pierre-Alex?"

"No!"

When I first suspected my wife of having an affair, I had indeed shared with Efelia the fact that it was a possibility. When she confirmed it, I had told Efelia that Mia had a French lover. I could not let my wife know that I had talked about this to my friend. It is true that she has asked me more than once not to share details of our private life with Efelia. So I lied.

Mia was quick to decide: "She seems to have a new-found audacity and it must be that she knows something about me. You are sure you didn't tell her?"

This time I shook my head. Women's intuition is strong. Somehow Mia already knew that Efelia knew about her affair.

"Well, I will not reply to her letter. I'm done with her. After trying for so long to be sensitive to her situation, I'm fed up! Enough is enough!"

Harboring negative emotions wasn't serving us. I asked Mia to let go of her anger towards Efelia and to forgive her one more time.

"Why do you always want me to make peace with her? Why do I have to swallow everything this girl tries to shove down my throat? Don't you understand that I have reached my limit?"

"For Sabrina's sake", I begged. "Make peace and forgive her because of Sabrina."

17

Spiritual realization

After spending a few months in Texas, Jean-Paul's company transferred us a second time to Venezuela. This time we would be living in the capital city of Caracas where Efelia and Sabrina lived. When this expatriate assignment was offered to Jean-Paul, he gladly welcomed the opportunity to be close to his little girl for an entire year.

Initially I had serious reservations about moving to Caracas. The mere thought of living in the same city as his "Venezuelan family", as Jean-Paul called them, put me in a state of near panic. However, I realized that I needed to complete the healing process started nearly six years ago, and make peace with our circumstances.

I had little contact with Sabrina's mother. Jean-Paul wanted me to show more compassion towards her but her arrogant behavior since the sleepover incident didn't encourage a close relationship between us. It had become apparent to both Jean-Paul and me that she would not hesitate to use their young daughter to obtain what she wanted from him. Had she not written to me that she would "disappear from our lives" since it seemed to be what I wanted! I would only make an effort to get along with Efelia for Sabrina's benefit and to please Jean-Paul.

We searched for the ideal apartment in one of the safest neighborhoods of the city, Altamira. We had been warned about the lack of security in Caracas; kidnappings were still common, and robberies frequent. Our twenty-first floor apartment at the Four Seasons Complex on Plaza Francia was a welcome oasis in the chaos of the city.

Our penthouse unit boasted a fabulous view of the Avila Mountain with its most famous landmark, the Humboldt Hotel on one side, and on the other, the city's hilly suburbs, islands of green amidst disparate office and apartment buildings. I never could tire of the impressive view from our terrace, particularly after sunset when millions of lights glittered along the Cota Mil, the *autopista* (expressway) along the Avila, and among the shantytowns built on the city's outskirts.

The lights created the illusion that this third world capital could be as prosperous as the City of Lights! Even the obelisk on Plaza Francia tried to measure up to Place de la Concorde. The city that never sleeps vibrated with an energy that translated into a perpetual noise late into the night. Caracas was a city of contrasts where rich neighborhoods adjoined clusters of rundown *barrios* (quarters).

Efelia and her son Sergio often came to the Four Seasons with Sabrina on weekends to enjoy the pool. They all loved to swim, and Efelia was very good at the sport. They also joined us occasionally for dinner. Sometimes we would order a pizza, or I'd prepare an easy meal for all of us. For a while we all seemed to be getting along. Soon Jean-Paul was able to bring Sabrina to our home without either her mother or her brother being present. Jean-Paul was happy to finally spend time with his daughter away from Efelia. We had bought her a Barbie bedroom set complete with a tent-like canopy, a hamper and matching twin bed covers. Jean-Paul installed the pink canopy in our guest room which became Sabrina's room. We hung her pictures on the walls, her books went inside the bedside cabinets and her toys decorated the room. The first time she saw it, she burst into tears. Maybe she thought we were going to have her move in with us? It took her several weeks to acclimate herself to the idea of sleeping over but she resigned herself, after we told her that her brother could come as well. Some nights, Jean-Paul would fall asleep in the other bed, while reading them a story.

His little girl was getting to be more at ease with Jean-Paul even though she was not very demonstrative of her affection for him. She would never hug him or say to him what he wanted to hear: "*¡Te quiero, Papa!*" (I love you, Dad). She always called him by his Spanish name: Pablo.

The first time she hugged him she made him promise he would not tell her mother. She made the same request from him the day she told him she loved him *un poquito* (a little bit).

"*¡Por favor no lo digas a mi mamá!*" (Please don't say anything to my mother).

It hurt Jean-Paul to see such resistance on the part of his daughter to show her feelings for him. He rarely shared with me his pain and his disappointment yet I knew what dilemma it was for him to have to fight so hard to gain his daughter's confidence. Jean-Paul was very determined to reach the goals he had set for Sabrina and nothing would prevent him from succeeding: She would become more independent of the mother, she would love and accept him as her father. She would be more affectionate towards him.

We both knew that she loved him; it was obvious in the way she held onto him when they walked together, in the way she jumped in his arms when he put her on a higher ground, or when they played at the pool. And she never tired of listening to the stories he read to her in Spanish from her favorite books.

I knew that she loved me too. She just would not say it nor would she ever give me a kiss, even though in the Venezuelan culture, everybody kisses everybody: your doctor, your massage therapist, your hairdresser all welcome you with a kiss on the cheek. But not Sabrina!

There were times when Jean-Paul wanted to be alone with his daughter. He was gone to the field for his job all week long, and on weekends I wanted to visit the countryside with him. He, on the other hand, just wanted to stay in the city with Sabrina. I often sat near the pool of the Four Seasons alone with a book while the two of them went to the nearby park or to a movie. I was thankful that I didn't have to go with them to the amusement centers where they often spent hours weekend after weekend.

Jean-Paul was encouraging me to go visit my daughters or my friends in the US, so he could enjoy his daughter all to himself! At times I felt excluded and wondered why my husband wanted me out of the way. I was starting to experience a deep resentment, due to the fact that Jean-Paul continued to speak to Sabrina's mother almost every single day.

"You should be talking to your daughter, instead of talking to the mother," I'd tell him. He didn't think that his daughter would listen to him on the phone. It is true that she had a short attention span, as she was only 5 or 6 years-old. He should be more patient with her and call anyway, even to just say "*¡Hola! ¿Que tal?*"

We had been in Venezuela several months when Sabrina made a comment that triggered a major upset between Jean-Paul and me. It was a Sunday afternoon and when they came back from the pool, I noticed that Jean-Paul's toenails needed a clipping and when I started doing it, Sabrina told me that I should not do it because her mother would do it for him! I was stunned.

"*¿Qué dijiste, mi amor?*" (What did you say, my love?)

"Leave it so my mom can do it for him."

What was she talking about? When could this have taken place?

"What do you want to say to this, Jean-Paul?"

"This is from such a long time ago. This little one has an amazing memory."

"Did the mother clip your toenails? In front of her daughter? I wonder why I'm finding out about this now! Why didn't you ever tell me?"

I was beginning to hyperventilate. I could feel my heart palpitating.

"Because it wasn't a big deal. The mother saw my feet at the pool and said I needed to clip my toenails. And she offered to do it for me."

"Jean-Paul, you NEVER allow anyone to touch your feet. You never want to get a professional pedicure. How could you let Efelia clip your toenails?"

"What's the big deal? She wanted to do it. She has this thing about nails. She can't stand long nails and always wants to cut even my finger-nails."

I couldn't help but wonder if my husband had any idea what nail clippings could be used for. Weren't hair and nail clippings used in unthinkable but common pagan behavior to cast spells? Why was I even thinking about this now? The thoughts were racing ...

Could it be what she had used to entrap him? It would explain his obsessive behavior when it came to both his daughter and the mother. It would explain the daily calls to Efelia that were still upsetting me, the uneasy feeling in my stomach every time I thought of their relationship. There was this quickening of the heart that warned me of something not quite right. I had tried to ignore the signs, to quiet the little voice inside my head. I kept praying that when we'd leave Venezuela, everything would go back to normal.

Every friend I had confided in about the situation had commented that the relationship Jean-Paul kept with Efelia was not a normal thing. And I agreed with them. Even though I had reassured myself that their exchanges were mostly about their young daughter, I knew she was confiding in him about practically everything in her life. Jean-Paul had told me that he was the only friend she had and that he would be "very upset" if I prevented him from keeping his friendship with her. Why did I feel my throat tightening and my guts twisting every time he'd mention her name?

The changes I had noticed in my husband came to mind. He appeared less relaxed than usual, more elusive, more preoccupied. He had started lying to me about insignificant things and at times, I didn't recognize the person he had become. His outbursts were also more frequent. On the few occasions when Jean-Paul would lose his temper, he would say very hurtful things to me. I chose to ignore them even though they had wounded me.

I was also thinking of Efelia's letter after they had all slept together at the hotel. It was right around the time when he had let her clip his toenails.

Why couldn't she leave my husband alone? Why couldn't she find herself a boyfriend? In the six years that I'd known her, I'd not once heard Jean-Paul say that she was dating. That was not normal! Was she waiting for me to leave my husband so she could have him?

When Efelia came to pick up her daughter at our apartment, I let her know I had found out about the nail clipping incident.

"I can't believe what your daughter told me today."

She smiled a fake smile. I could see she was embarrassed. I calmly stated that unless she is a professional in a beauty salon, a woman who is not intimate with a man has no business clipping his toenails. She didn't reply anything, keeping a fixed smirk of a smile on her face. Jean-Paul told me that when they spoke the next day she asked him if I was very angry. Of course she knew that I would be! This woman was disturbing the harmony between my husband and me and I had called her out on her game!

"I didn't dare tell her what reaction you had to this small incident."

"Well, thank you, but I'm sure she knows. Anyway, I've told you enough times that you don't need to share what happens between us with her. You don't need to tell her about our life! And that was not a small incident. If it were so meaningless, you would have mentioned it to me, don't you think? It's because you knew how I would react that you never brought it up!"

"It was nearly three years ago. Do you think I was even thinking about it? It meant nothing to me."

"It must have made an impression on Sabrina if she can remember it so well. She was only three years old! I wonder if the mother asked you not to say anything to me. She must have known how much it would disturb me."

"Why are you always looking for something bad in her? Why can't you just get over the past? You still cannot forgive her, after all this time?"

"Jean-Paul, you know that I have forgiven Efelia a long time ago. You know it, she knows it and most importantly: I know it. I simply cannot understand the degree of intimacy you still maintain with her. There is no degree of friendship I can think of that would make me clip the toenails of any man I know. And I have some very close male friends!"

How could Jean-Paul accuse me of lacking forgiveness towards his friend? I prayed every single day for peace, love, joy, forgiveness. I did not hold grudges. I only wanted to set boundaries and have them respected. There were limits to my level of tolerance!

I remembered Earl Nightingale's message in *The Strangest Secret* that Jean-Paul and I have shared with our daughters and with many of our friends: "You are what you think about!" And I had also learned to affirm, in the present tense, powerful and personal affirmations to which I would add both action and conviction!

I got on my mini trampoline on our terrace and chanted: "I am Joy, I am Love, I am Faith, I am Happiness, I am Courage, I am Resilience, I am Harmony, I am Forgiveness." Over and over I would remind myself of these qualities I possessed that would help me overcome any adversity. This was a great exercise, one that I had often recommended to others in my workshops.

I also got into my 'voodoo mood' as Jean-Paul jokingly referred to all the Feng Shui rituals I had incorporated in my everyday life: I surrounded myself with fresh flowers and classical music. I lit candles and rang bells, sprayed alcohol to cleanse the energies around our apartment. I reminded myself that no one could make me feel sad without my consent. I was still the happiest woman I knew. Nothing would get me down!

◆   ◆   ◆

Shortly after the nail-clipping incident, on a Friday evening, Jean-Paul called me right around the time I expected him to be home.

"Hi, I'm about an hour away from Caracas and I'd like to stop for a few minutes to see my daughter."

"Okay, dinner will be ready by the time you get here. I'll see you later."

He was returning from Valencia, a two-hour drive from Caracas with our driver Juan Carlos. A couple of minutes after he had called, I tried Jean-Paul on his cell phone and couldn't get through. I then called the driver and asked to speak to Señor Pablo. Juan Carlos started mumbling something about being at a café eating his dinner and admitted that Señor Pablo was not with him.

I called Jean-Paul's cell phone again. It went to his voicemail. After about forty minutes, I was finally able to reach him and asked where he was: "I've just arrived at the apartment and am playing with my daughter."

"What do you mean you've just arrived? I spoke to Juan Carlos nearly an hour ago and you weren't with him. What's going on?"

"We arrived earlier than I had anticipated."

"Jean-Paul, please tell me the truth. You were already at their place when you called, weren't you? I cannot believe that you lied to me about that! Why couldn't you tell me?"

Silence was his only reply.

"Do you want to know why I was calling you? I wanted you to bring Sabrina to have dinner with us. Why are you lying to me?" I shouted that last question.

I slammed the phone before he could answer, picked up my purse and went out, leaving my cell phone in evidence on the kitchen counter. Dinner was on the stove, the table was set for three.

I walked up the street to the Celarg Theater and bought a ticket for the 8 pm performance of the popular show: "Women over 30." It distracted me for the next couple of hours from the feeling of sadness, anger, insecurity and helplessness this latest episode had left me with. Had I been so naïve as to trust my husband to always tell me the truth only to be deceived by his lies? I was fuming when I left the apartment. The show was a welcome diversion.

When I got back home, I went straight to my computer to write an e-mail to Delphine and empty my heart of the deception experienced earlier.

Jean-Paul had not eaten his dinner. He may have apologized but I was not in a receptive mood and ignored his invitation to come and eat with him. When he went to bed, I was still at the computer and kept silent. I enclosed myself inside my virtual protective shield to lessen the feeling of despondency I was starting to experience again.

I was hurt; I was disappointed. I was surprised that my husband couldn't even trust me with a simple admission like his visit to his daughter. Granted, I didn't like it when he stayed in their apartment for too long. It gave the impression of a happy family, and since I was never invited there, I felt that his place wasn't there either. I didn't mind him picking his daughter up but I didn't like when he waited for the mother to come home from work so he could visit with her as well. Yes, that was probably the jealous wife in me reacting to a circumstance towards which I still harbored resentment. I resented being excluded from their little circle. I resented that he kept a somewhat secret life. I was becoming once again suspicious and was wondering about the state of our relationship.

One time, when Sabrina had asked him in front of me why he couldn't live with her mother and her, Jean-Paul had replied: "Because I live with Mia."

I didn't think that was a good answer. If he didn't live with me, would he be with Efelia? He should tell his daughter the truth: he does not belong with his mother. He is married to me. Can a six year-old even understand all this?

At breakfast, I asked my husband if he had anything to say about the previous evening.

"It was just a little lie: I wanted to see my daughter for more than five minutes, so I lied about how long I was spending there. Do you know why I didn't tell you the truth? It's because I wasn't sure how you would react. You get upset so easily I never know how to deal with you!"

"But why? Have I not been supportive of you all these years? I think I deserve better. I frankly don't understand why you're acting this way. Do you want me to leave you so you can have your freedom?"

"I didn't want to upset you. I know this was stupid of me but I did it because I know you don't like when I stay there too long."

"And don't you realize you make it worse when you hide the truth? It makes me wonder what else you hide from me."

"I'm not hiding anything from you. I just feel that you sometimes treat me like a child who will be punished if I don't do exactly as told. I'm a grown-up man, Mia. Let me be myself. Let me be with my daughter when I want, for however long I want. Stop being the captain of the world!"

I reminded myself once again of what truly mattered; the love that we had for one another. I could empathize with Jean-Paul for feeling the way he did. I wanted to always decide how my husband should live his life. It was time to let go, and show more fluidity. We were able to get over this incident rather quickly. Jean-Paul apologized, said he had been stupid. I forgave him, and said I had been too possessive.

◆   ◆   ◆

The following Monday was Halloween. I called Efelia to say I would pick up Sabrina at her school and take her to the San Ignacio shopping center where Jean-Paul's office was located. Since Jean-Paul wanted to see his daughter so badly he had to lie about it, I decided to surprise my husband. The three of us had lunch together. When I mentioned to Jean-Paul that he should tell our driver where Efelia's office was located so we could drop Sabrina there, his split-second hesitation clued me on the fact that Juan Carlos already knew where Efelia worked. And if he did, it was because he had picked her up there with my husband; and that meant that they had gone out to lunch together. He had never told me about it. But I instantly knew. So I asked him, and he admitted: "It was for her birthday."

"And you couldn't tell me?"

"I didn't want to upset you."

"What is happening to you? Are you starting to get the message that when you lie to me I get more upset than when you tell me the truth? Do you also realize that I end up finding out the truth? Do you know how much I detest lies and being taken for a fool?"

"No one is taking you for a fool."

"Really? When you bring our driver into your little secrets, isn't that making me look like a fool? Frankly, my dear, my level of tolerance is being tested big time. I don't understand why you are being so secretive all of a sudden."

"It's because I knew how you would react. You are making a scene now and it's something that happened last month."

"I don't think there would have been any scene if you had just told me about it. Thanks for trusting my reaction! Now you make me wonder why you needed to hide the fact that you had lunch with her! Do you understand the power you give Efelia when you make this lunch a secret between the two of you? You have NO consideration for my feelings!"

Every time an incident such as this one took place, I would feel a knot right in the center of my chest; a tightness that caused me great discomfort. It also set me back in my efforts to keep our relationship healthy. I would keep my positive attitude and my upbeat expectancy that all would turn out for the best, but I could feel my energy being vacuumed right out of my body. I would pray in front of my altar: "Dear God, please give me the necessary strength to go through this ordeal. Guide me; tell me what I should do. I want to save my marriage. I want to regain faith in my husband. Please help me!"

It couldn't be a simple twist of fate that these three distinct incidents had occurred almost simultaneously. I had prayed for clarity. What was the meaning of all this? Should I be alarmed? I prayed with more fervor than ever.

I had brought Doreen Virtue's Goddess Guidance cards with me to Caracas. I had never used them before. I had heard Doreen speak at a spiritual conference in Las Vegas a few months earlier, and her book *Healing with the Angels* was one I often consulted. I decided to do a reading with my brand new cards. I prepared myself as instructed, blessed the deck and pulled three cards randomly; indicating the past, the present and the future. The card representing the future was giving me a clear message: "Stop worrying. Everything is going to be fine … There are no blocks or obstacles in your way, except your own projections of fear into your future … Clear your heart of fear and replace those energies with ones that will serve you and your family instead. Refuse to think of anything except your bright today and tomorrow."

This message must have been written for me! What an amazing 'coincidence' that I should pull the card most appropriate for my circumstances! I decided to follow the advice on the card. In addition, I meditated more often, repeated the prayer of St. Francis of Assisi both in the morning when I first awoke and before retiring at night:

"Lord, make me an instrument of your peace.
Where there is hatred, let me sow love.
Where there is injury, pardon.
Where there is discord, harmony.
Where there is doubt, faith,
Where there is despair, hope,
Where there is darkness, light,
And where there is sadness, help me bring JOY!

Grant that I may seek
Not so much to be consoled as to console others;
Not so much to be forgiven as to forgive others;
No so much to be loved as to love others,
Because it is in forgiving that we are forgiven,
In loving that we are loved
And in dying that we are born to Eternal Life."

I focused more and more on what I wanted, less on what I feared. I asked myself if the very fact that I was obsessing over my husband's excessive attachment to Sabrina's family wasn't actually increasing this attachment. I had heard someone say that what we resist persists, and I resolved to completely let go of my fears and allow God's will to be done. During my meditation, I bathed myself in the divine light and extended to the world the blessings I was receiving from the universe. I would include Efelia in my prayers and send her blessings of light, peace, forgiveness, compassion, and even of love!

I was getting tired of the constant assault on my peace of mind because of the relationship between Jean-Paul and his 'other family.' Our frequent arguments were draining me of my energy.

When I confided in her, my friend psychologist Beatriz offered this comment:

"Your husband needs to realize that the sense of guilt he still carries with him should not be channeled through you. When he asks you to entertain in your home the mother of his little girl, it's because he feels guilty. You cannot become part of his guilt trip. You should have nothing to do with this woman. Your home is your sacred space. She doesn't belong there."

Beatriz was expressing what I was feeling without wanting to fully acknowledge it: I didn't feel comfortable having Efelia in our home. Not even when she came to pick up her daughter. From the very beginning of our stay in Caracas, I had told Jean-Paul that she might be envious of our lifestyle. She was of a modest social condition and could resent witnessing how we lived. His reply was that I didn't know her as well as he did and that he was sure it wasn't the case.

Beatriz helped me articulate what I felt deep inside of my heart: that I could no longer tolerate the daily phone calls between my husband and Efelia, and that I should no longer invite her in our home. It had nothing to do with being selfish. I was sure that this was best for me in order to experience peace.

I finally had the courage to ask Jean-Paul to respect the boundaries I wanted to redefine, by honoring my wish. I wanted to distance myself from Efelia, and not have her in the privacy of our home any longer.

He was away in the field and we were speaking on the telephone when I asked him if he had a few minutes:

"Darling, I need your support in a decision I've made. I know that it was important to you that I get along with Sabrina's mother. And you know how hard I have tried these past few years. What I feel deep inside every time you speak of her or you speak to her in front of me is a clear indication to me that something is not right. I do not feel good inside. I don't trust her manipulative tactics. I don't like the fact that nearly all our arguments stem from something related to her. I want to regain the inner peace I treasure. I don't want to speak to her, and I don't want her in our home. I hope you understand. I've prayed a lot about it and I'm asking for your support in my decision. That is the only way I can reestablish harmony in our life."

It was true that lately every fight between us was triggered by something Efelia did or said and it felt like she was a third leg in our relationship. Maybe all that was needed was to distance ourselves from her. Of course Jean-Paul couldn't completely avoid her. If he would call her less often and from his office rather than from our home, I told him I would greatly appreciate it. I didn't want to pretend any more that she could ever be my friend. I felt no hatred in my heart towards her and it was probably not intentional on her part to cause such turmoil in our life. Yet there was no denying that she had triggered too many feuds between us. Jean-Paul had to acknowledge the fact that we had experienced some major shifts in our relationship. He would defend her vehemently every time I made the slightest remark about her and since I had no one to defend me, I felt at a disadvantage. I tended to ignore Jean-Paul's comments but at the soul level, I was hurting.

18

Mixed emotions (Efelia)

Pablo and Mia came back to live here in my city when Sabrina was almost five years old. It wasn't easy to face him and his wife together in front of my friends. Even my mother and my son's godfather met Mia one day when she and Pablo were bringing Sabrina back home. That was embarrassing. I was reminded in front of my mother that I had a second child out of wedlock and this time with a married man. And there they were both of them together in front of my family and my friends. It was like an accusation.

When they first arrived in Caracas, they both noticed that my daughter was extremely shy and that she lacked confidence. The first time we were meeting them at their hotel I had not warned Sabrina that Mia was with her father. She knew Mia from the pictures but she was too young to remember the last time she had seen her in person. So she started to cry as soon as she saw Mia, and she refused to say hello to them. If his wife had let him be alone with us, then maybe my daughter would not have had this reaction.

We went out together the first few weekends that they were here because Sabrina was still very upset when I asked her to stay by herself with them. I apologized for my daughter's behavior and Mia said that she understood: Sabrina was used to seeing her father alone; when she appeared at his side, she was "the other woman", and my daughter didn't understand what was going on. It was true that the last few times that

Pablo visited us in Caracas, we had been like a family. It was a fantasy that gave my children and me great joy, even though I knew that it was an illusion!

On one occasion, when we were at a shopping mall, I told Pablo that I didn't like the tone of voice Mia had used with me. She was talking down to me. She may have felt superior because she was his wife, and maybe she wondered what right I had to be enjoying her husband's friendship and his generosity. But she did not need to have this attitude when talking to me.

I thought that maybe what bothered her was the fact that her husband had bought us the apartment. I had told Pablo I would need to move out of my mother's house when I became pregnant. He decided to buy the apartment. He said it was for his daughter. Every time he came with her to pick up Sabrina, it made me feel ashamed, because his wife could see that I now lived in a better place, thanks to her husband's generosity. He's the one who insisted that his daughter should be in a safer neighborhood. I could never invite her inside the apartment. They lived in such a spectacular place and mine was very humble. They helped us furnish it with some of their furniture that they were not using. They also gave us a rug and a computer. I was grateful for their generosity but at the same time, it made me feel like I owed them something.

When Pablo told me that he wanted his daughter to go to a bilingual school, I said that the school was very expensive. I was sending Sergio there with almost everything I was earning at my job. I did that because I was living with my mother. Pablo said he was going to take care of this. He was being very generous and I thanked him all the time for his gifts to his daughter. Mia also bought many presents for my daughter. She said that Sabrina was like a granddaughter.

When Sabrina was a baby, Mia seemed to accept my daughter and myself better than she did this time around. We were like two normal women having a conversation when we first met. I was welcome in their home. That seemed too crazy to be true. I used to think it was *una bella locura,* (a beautiful madness!) She seemed to be a woman full of wisdom, who understood what love was, and who could accept a situation other women could not.

Then she seemed to become jealous of the love her husband had for my family. As if that love was taking something away from his love for her. Sometimes, I observed how she reacted when he came to see us alone in Caracas. She was very jealous.

For a woman as educated as she was, I told her she was not acting as "Motivation in Action", the acronym for her name. After a visit from Pablo when he had invited us to spend the night in his hotel room, she wrote to me that I should never accept another invitation from her husband for such an arrangement.

I replied that if she was making such a big deal out of this, it indicated that she didn't want him to see his little girl anymore. That was it! I asked her where she had obtained my e-mail address and why she was writing to me at my office. I told her that she was wasting her time and my time with such *tontería* (stupidity). I was upset because she made it sound like I was still involved with her husband. She got mad and Pablo was mad also. It hurt me to see how Pablo was siding with his wife on a matter we had both agreed was no big deal. He said I had no right to address his wife in this manner. He made me send a letter of excuse. I told her in the letter that I felt like a tigress who was protecting her baby. What I did was for my daughter. Mia never wrote to me after that.

We seldom spoke on the telephone even when they were living in Caracas. When we did, the conversation was brief. It was either because Sabrina was sick, or because Mia wanted to make plans for their weekends with my daughter. We also had conversations when we went out together with Pablo and my two children. She often said that she and Pablo had no secrets for one another and that if I didn't want him to know something I should not tell her!

◆   ◆   ◆

After they had been in Caracas for about a year, Pablo wanted his daughter to obtain an American passport and he asked me to go to the U.S. Embassy in Caracas with him and Sabrina. I was shocked when the assistant to the U.S. Consul asked me the questions about my relationship with Pablo. Even to my close girlfriends I never had to give such details about what took place between us. I felt as if they were going through my private journals and were reading my secrets. I told Pablo and Mia this was very embarrassing. Pablo felt the same way since they asked similar questions of him. We had to go back because they were not satisfied with their investigation. They wanted proof that we had been lovers! They wanted proof that he was the father!

The test that Pablo could take to check his DNA was a possibility, but they wanted him to pay several hundreds of dollars for it. They also wanted one of their workers to be there when the test was being done. Pablo refused. That day when they interrogated me in front of several other people and in front of my daughter was one of the worst days of my life. If they wanted proof, I would show them every journal entry, every letter we exchanged, every receipt from the places we visited together, the movie theater tickets, everything I was saving to show my daughter one day so she would know that she had not been born out of a one night stand.

When we went back for the final interview at the embassy, they no longer demanded more proof. Pablo had asked Mia if she would be willing to show them her own journal entries where she mentioned our relationship. I was praying that this would not happen. It would have been too embarrassing.

During the time that the application was being processed, I asked myself what it would mean for my daughter to have a U.S. passport. Was Pablo planning to kidnap her from me and give her a better life in North

America? Was he going to show her such a good life there that she might not want to live here in Venezuela anymore?

I knew that there was a lack of stability in my country. The violence was scary. The crimes in the street, the robberies of private homes, the kidnappings were all part of our every day life. Pablo wanted a safer life for his little girl. But I made him promise that he wouldn't take her away from me.

When the passport was ready, I had mixed feelings about what it meant and could barely express any satisfaction at seeing that my daughter had been recognized as an American citizen. Pablo admitted to me that he was quite surprised by my reaction. I was thinking how fortunate Sabrina was and at the same time how scary it was that she could one day leave her country and her family and move to North America!

◆   ◆   ◆

During their time in Venezuela, Pablo insisted on visiting with his daughter on both Saturdays and Sundays, weekend after weekend. He said he would only be in Caracas a few more months. It was always "a few more months." It turned out to be nearly two years! On some occasions, I simply went out with my two children, and didn't take my cellular phone with me and he would call and not find us anywhere. He would be very angry with me and I felt bad but I worked late hours during the week and I wanted to spend time with my children on the weekends as well.

When he took her for a five-day trip to Disney World, I missed my daughter very much and prayed that she would behave well and not cry while she was gone. The pictures they took showed me that she had a great time. She also met her grandfather and Pablo's brother in Florida. Even though they spoke a little Spanish to her, Pablo told me that Sabrina did not say one word to them when she visited his family. She could be very stubborn, very strong-willed for a child of her age.

It was difficult for me to observe how Sabrina was separating herself from me, how she was growing up and becoming more independent. She had been my little baby for so long. I had nursed her past the age of four. She slept in my bed with me. She was my queen, my little princess, my love. I did not want her to say to me one day that she loved her father more than she loved me. My son Sergio had nearly broken my heart by admitting to me that he loved his godfather more than he loved me! I had made myself a promise: my daughter would never say something so hurtful to me. She would love me more than she would love anyone else.

I was not ashamed of how I felt in my heart. It was not easy to stop loving a man as extraordinary as Pablo. I was raising my two children with pride. I wanted them to be proud of their mother when they became older.

19

Inner transformation

Chloe and Malcolm were married in Maui at our 'up-country' property in Kula. The gardens of our family estate provided the perfect setting!

Kula is known for its rainy climate but on the morning of the wedding, the first day of the Summer solstice, the clouds started dissipating as soon as Roland, the minister from New Zealand began the ceremony.

We had unobstructed views of both West Maui Mountain and the coast. The wedding was a wonderful expression of love. Delightful moments filled everyone's heart with joy, love and awe: The blessing of the rings, the singing in both Hawaiian and Maori, the circling of family and friends around the couple at the end of the exchange of vows, dancing barefoot on the grass, singing Haitian and French songs after the DJ left, lingering under the tent to watch the sunset. Our entire 'Hawaiian family' had gathered for the occasion: three of my brothers and their wives, my sister, our auntie Mamiline, two of my nieces, my nephew James and his sweetheart, as well as our daughter Suzanna, our dear friend Delphine who is like a sister to me, and Malcolm's nephew David and his girlfriend who had all flown to Maui for the occasion. Danielle and her husband Michael who had gotten engaged in Maui the previous year were expecting their first offspring in a few weeks and couldn't join us for the celebration. We were eagerly expecting the birth of our first grandbaby. We were so proud of our youngest: after several years taking her daily dosage of anti-depressant, she had completely weaned herself from the Wellbutrin. We called them right after the exchange of vows so that they could participate a little in the festivities!

When I toasted the newlyweds I expressed my wish that they'd be as happy as Jean-Paul and I had been for the past 34 years, then I corrected myself: "I wish you to be even happier, you deserve it!" Although we have been very happy Jean-Paul and I, there was still a shadow between us. I was aware of it, and I knew that it would soon dissipate, just like the clouds that formed a perfect backdrop for the pictures during the marriage ceremony had been replaced by a beautiful sunshine during the reception that followed.

The *pupus* (Hawaiian appetizers) served by the caterer were delicious and plentiful, the DJ's choice of music perfect. Everyone had a great time and I was a proud mother of the bride and a very happy wife to my handsome husband. We all look radiant in the pictures, wearing identical plumeria leis, a symbol of both resilience—a cut branch, when it has fallen to the ground starts a new plumeria tree—and of connectedness: the tightly woven flowers symbolize beauty, harmony and wholeness.

This wedding had brought us closer together and Jean-Paul and I couldn't stop marveling at how this day was surely the most wonderful of our lives, second only to our own wedding day 34 years prior. Love was in everyone's heart. There were many loving couples there, and it felt like we were all falling in love all over again. Weddings often have this effect. When dancing with my husband, I could feel in the way he squeezed me in his arms that he was reclaiming me as his wife. He had probably feared losing me when I had my French adventure. We both had dealt with our tribulations and we were now recommitting to one another. Without formally expressing it, we were renewing our own vows.

A few days after the wedding, we drove up to the Haleakala volcano to watch the sunset. I was carrying a symbolic white rose to offer in exchange for the one wish I would be making when we reached the summit.

I had prayed about it, and invoked the Father/Mother God, the Virgin Mary, her Son Jesus the Christ, the Angels, the Archangels, all my guides, and even KuanYin.

"Who's Kuan Yin, now?" Jean-Paul had asked when I mentioned her name.

"She's an Eastern goddess of nurturing love and purity. She's protecting women and children. I am putting my wish into her care."

When I threw my white rose inside the crater, I just said: "It is in God's hands."

On a piece of paper that I had wrapped around the thorns of the rose I had written: "BRING MY HUSBAND BACK TO ME!"

Even though I had noticed my husband's renewed love and he had reassured me that he was still in love with me, there was still a lingering shadow of uneasiness when it came to his relationship with his Venezuelan family. I continued to pray daily, trusting that the uncertainty that still assailed me would soon dissolve. We'd be leaving Caracas before the end of the year. I could not wait to be back in the US for good, away from that environment.

◆　　　◆　　　◆

Back in Caracas, I read a lot and swam often. I went out with my girlfriends from the Four Seasons and enjoyed weekly massages with my wonderful masseuse Araselis. I went to the theater or to open air concerts held weekly at the PDVSA Park conveniently located a short walking distance from the Four Seasons complex. It was a good life. It was a wonderful opportunity for me to enjoy the culture of a country that I had at times hated, but that I would probably miss once we would return home to Texas.

During my meditations I often recalled an amazing healing session I had after an injury sustained while I was dancing. My left knee had snapped, perhaps it was a ligament. The pain was such that I could not walk on the leg and I had to use a wheelchair for a couple of days, badly limping afterwards.

Several weeks had gone by since my knee injury. I had an MRI in Caracas and was supposed to start physical therapy, after a scheduled trip to California. I had to cancel my yoga classes and even swimming had become a strain. In early March, I was on my way to John Gray's ranch in Mendocino County to attend his Wellness and Nutrition seminar with my brother Dave and his fiancée Greta. We were picking up their friend Samantha in Berkeley to bring her there as well. Samantha introduced us to Jeffrey, a healer who had worked with her in Phoenix were she lived. As soon as Greta mentioned my knee, Jeffrey started working on me right there in the middle of the parking lot. He used techniques I recognized from the Pranic Healing method Marianna had used. After about 20 minutes, I experienced something that is difficult to put in words. First my body slowly bent forward at the waist, as if to acknowledge a master. Then it bent backwards. I had 3 people behind me: my brother, his fiancée and Samantha. I sensed that they were there to catch me if I went too far back—which I didn't.

It was around 11:00 in the morning, under a clear blue sky, and bright sunshine. Cars were cruising by, pedestrians were strolling along and joggers were running nearby. Yet for me, it was as if the rest of the world had ceased to matter. I heard nothing but Jeffrey's voice, mentioning resentment being at the root of the injury.

"She needs to get rid of the past; of things that upset her and she needs to release. Release left knee, left foot. Nice, nice … Release blockage in the eyes: something she doesn't want to see. There's a blockage in the ears, she doesn't want to know …"

He was gesturing with the right hand, in quick, sharp moves, dragging out the disease and "throwing" it to the ground, to an imaginary fire or a bucket of water.

I felt totally at peace, floating slightly above ground, smiling, enjoying the soothing, calming notion of serenity, harmony, peace, and well being that was enveloping me.

All of a sudden, my right hand shot right up towards a point in the sky. Behind my closed eyes, I 'saw' the most amazing, luminous, clear, dazzling, blinding light I have ever known to exist! It shone so much I thought I might be looking straight into the sun. It was electrifying! I saw an aqua blue spread of rays coming from that light. It was euphoric. I felt pure bliss. My hand moved towards Samantha first, then Jeffrey. The rays seemed to come out of the tip of my fingers. Tears rolled down on both cheeks.

It was an experience I could never forget. The light was so bright it might have come from another realm. It was vibrating, swirling inwards, and it was of an intensity never experienced before or since.

I didn't want to come back to the reality of the parking lot of this Berkeley field. I was pointing towards the point in the sky where the light was, shaking my head in disbelief, smiling and crying all at the same time.

"Oh ... my ... God!!! This ... light!!!" is all I could say.

Time stood still, I lost all notion of it. Then, Jeffrey was calling me. He was bringing me back to my surroundings. I was coming out of a trance. It took me several moments before I could open my eyes. When I finally did, I bowed my head slightly to Jeffrey, and then turned to Dave, Greta and Samantha. My face was still moist from the tears. Their faces were glowing in the sun. I noticed they each had a gold patch on their foreheads, like a light. I reached out, asking them what they thought it could be. It was shaped differently on each forehead. It was the same color, though. Bright gold. Jeffrey didn't have one.

I also noticed that Dave, Greta and Samantha all had smiles on their faces, and they were all holding their hands in the same manner: all five fingers together, crossed flat on their chests, at the base of their neck. They had so much love pouring out of their eyes. It was surreal. I wondered what had just taken place.

Dave was the first one to speak:

"We were holding the space for you!"

"What does that mean?"

"It's okay. We held the space for you. You're okay. Go sit down, or lay down in the back seat of the car for a while."

He didn't have to say it twice. I wanted to continue basking in the moment. I also was suddenly exhausted and just wanted to sleep. I had read stories of people having near death experiences and seeing a bright light. I was fully alive! What gift had I just been given? A glimpse into the dimension of pure, divine love!

Later, I asked Samantha, who was sitting next to me in the car on the way to John Gray's ranch:

"Was I pointing at the sun when I was pointing at the light?"

"No, Mia, you were looking completely in the other direction."

"What do you think it was, then?"

"I'm not sure. But it seemed to have been beautiful, judging from the look on your face."

"That was the most amazing, the most surreal … It was not from this world!"

She just smiled.

"How is your knee?"

"I don't even know that I have a knee anymore. I've been bathed by this Light. I think I'm healed!"

Samantha and I spoke about my experience during the week we spent at John's ranch. I confided in her that nearly every time I meditated I saw a light behind my closed eyes. It took different colors, mostly indigo and purple. On occasion, it was magenta, or red or yellow. But never before had I seen "The Light!" This was the first time in my life that I had a glimpse of what I then knew was the beautiful realm that awaits us on the other side. I had 'seen' this beautiful pale turquoise color, and it was coming right out of the tips of my fingers, going towards the Light. I noticed the same color in the ocean later in the week, when we walked along the beach across from De Haven Inn where we were staying. It was the color that the waves formed when they folded. The color was only apparent for a short time. I asked Samantha what she called that color: "sea-foam." That was it! Sea-foam! That was the color bathing me while Jeffrey healed my knee.

After this experience, I wondered if I could use the same type of healing Jeffrey had used to take care of my emotional wounds. If I could just extract the leftover resentment and discontentment still experienced occasionally, wouldn't that be wonderful?

My friend Astrid who lived in Caracas was also a Pranic healer. As soon as I could, I had her work on me. With the help of my spiritual guides, we activated and accelerated the healing process. Astrid used rubbing alcohol to cleanse the energies in the area around my head and my heart. She would 'gather' them in a quick movement of the wrist and then 'throw away' in a bucket filled with water the emotions I wanted extracted from my psyche. With her left hand, she would 'measure' the energy to determine whether there was still resistance, indicating that the emotions were still lingering, or if the energy was flowing, indicating the healing was complete. I had a few sessions with her.

There are many different schools of faith healing besides Pranic Healing. In the Christian tradition, the Holy Spirit is often invoked when praying for a miraculous recovery. I do believe that miracles occur daily in answer to prayers regardless of faith or tradition. What is important is not the image or the name invoked so much as the energy summoned. No matter their tradition, saints are holy people. Beautiful Kuan Yin reminds me of the Virgin Mother. Krishna could be compared to the Christ. There are several paths to take us back to the one universal Source.

In addition to Jesus on his cross, and a beautiful reproduction of the *Madonna col Bambino* (Virgin and Child) by Filippo Lippi, on the wall above it, my healing table welcomes a statuette of Kuan Yin, a tiny laughing Buddha, and a few angels. I pray Angels and Archangels with fervor. I feel protected, especially by Gabrielle, the angel of communication. It is part of my tradition.

In my own family, on my mother's side, two miracles were widely talked about: the unexplainable recoveries from serious illnesses of both grandparents. One was even documented by medical doctors and the whole story was published in a physician's magazine back in the early 1920's. The family has always claimed that my grandfather's healing was an answer to prayers to St. Theresa. That's why the family home in Haiti is still known as *Villa Ste Thérèse*! My grandfather's head had swollen to a frightening dimension because of an eye condition. Surgery was scheduled. This was at a time when they had no penicillin. He had been on the operating table, ready to have one of his eyes surgically removed when the physician for no apparent reason decided to have one last test, which showed that the eye was now disease-free. Even though the doctors had diagnosed severe optical nerve damage, and the prognosis had been that he would lose the sight in his right eye, my grandfather was able to see perfectly well. His swollen head returned to normal. The only glasses Papi Denis ever wore were reading glasses. He read with both eyes, without effort until his death at the age of 97!

As for my grandmother, she was left crippled and wheelchair-bound after a month in bed following a pulmonary congestion, and several organ collapses. One of her legs became shorter than the other. She was sent to France to be treated and spent three and a half years there with her oldest daughter, first in Nice then in Paris. The boat trip had taken 21 days. Papi remained at home the entire time, having to work overtime to pay for the medical expenses, the trips and the *pensionnat* (boarding school) where my aunt was enrolled. After fervent prayers to the Virgin Mary, Mammie regained the use of both legs and never required crutches of any kind. Her promises in exchange for her full recovery were that she would go to Lourdes to give thanks, that she would never wear any frivolous jewelry until the end of her life, and that for two years, she would wear a plain white dress made of very common calico material. She was healed. She kept her promises. She visited Lourdes before going back to Haiti. The white calico dress was her uniform for two years. I don't remember her wearing bright colors until her death at 93. The only jewelry she wore besides her wedding band was a gold charm of Mother Mary whom she thanked daily! She even gave away her engagement ring to the daughter who went to France with her.

My 95 year-old aunt is the daughter who lived in France and who was now praying the saints for me. She seemed to have a direct connection with many spiritual guides, especially St. Jude, known as *"patron des causes désespérées"* (the saint of hopeless situations) in the Catholic faith. I had confided in her that we needed a miracle and she was praying for Jean-Paul and me.

Once I had decided to completely surrender to the Divine, my heart felt lighter, I started singing again, dancing more spontaneously, and jumping regularly on my trampoline. Life was once again an exciting adventure! My healing was progressing!

I continued praying, strongly believing and expecting that my husband would soon come back to me. I could tell he was not completely there for me. But I had faith in the outcome! I believed in miracles!

20

The transmutation (Jean-Paul)

I may not tell Mia very often but I am with her even though sometimes, it may appear that I'm not. I have not left her. I'm still with her. I still love her deeply. I have asked her to give me these next several weekends and allow me to dedicate them exclusively to my little girl. I work at the jobsite very far from Caracas during the week and I only get to see Sabrina on weekends. Mia sees my attachment to Sabrina as an obsession. She doesn't seem to realize that I only want to gain my little girl's affection and time is running out on me. Our stay in Venezuela will be over soon. I have set goals I haven't reached yet. I want to see my daughter more independent of her mother. I want her to be more comfortable with me, more affectionate. I want to take her to Disney World for a week. I want to win her love by my actions and affection towards her. My most fervent wish is to hear her one day tell me on her own that she loves me, without having to force her to say it. What wouldn't I give for her, just once, to jump and throw herself in my arms, and give me a real hug, full of love? When I meet our friend's children, they kiss and hug me and want to play with me. I see the demonstration of their love towards their parents as well and I silently pray that Sabrina would be more demonstrative with me.

I have spent time with her almost every single weekend that we were in Caracas. I have taken her to every amusement center in the city, to the zoo, to the movies, to the pool, to children shows, to her favorite restaurants. I probably have done more for my youngest than for any of my other daughters because she only has me for a short time. And time is running out on me. In just a few months, we will be going back home to Texas.

Throughout our stay in Caracas, Sabrina has never accepted a kiss from either Mia or me without fighting and "erasing" it from her cheek. Now she lets me kiss her but has refused any hug or kiss from Mia. She seems to fear that if she shows us any sign of affection, she is somehow betraying her mother. She behaves so differently when her mom is around. In her little head she cannot comprehend that I do not live with her and her mom. She sees her friends' parents together at her school and she wonders why I live with Mia and not with her.

Sabrina's most tender moments with me were probably when we went alone for a weekend to a water park on the island of Margarita. What fun we had. I was 7 years-old again. We spent two full days at the park. She wanted to show me how brave she was on those water slides, or how she could hold her breath under water. At night as we had to share a double bed she would cuddle up to me and I would put these tender moments in my emotional bank account, for later use when she would get back to her old ways and demonstrate less affection.

Once, Sabrina was very close to letting Mia kiss her but then she retracted herself and told us: "I don't want my *mamá* to know."

Mia has resigned herself and steals a hug here and there, when we play "cheese sandwich" with Sabrina and we squeeze her between the two of us.

I imagine that it must be hard for my wife to understand the love I have for my little girl. She must see Sabrina as an inconvenience, as a constant reminder of my straying seven years ago. I forget at times that it may be painful for her to recall all that she went through. I often wonder how I would feel toward Mia's baby if the roles were reversed. It is hard for me to imagine that I would not love her child even if I was not the father.

I know my wife's capacity to forgive and move forward. She has demonstrated it many times. She showed undeniable compassion towards Efelia from the beginning, and seemed to completely accept into her life, not only my little girl, but her brother and mother as well. I guess she was being heroic.

She now admits that she did it to please and appease me, and that there was also some fear that I might show my anger if she expressed her true feelings. She had initially defended Efelia to her family and friends. I heard her say to them that the girl was a decent person, that it could have been worse, and that we were able to all get along quite well. And for a while it had been like that. I may have asked a lot of her, but she always seemed to have a good time. I know she has acquired tools that allow her to deal with situations that others couldn't accept.

There were a few incidents that showed me how manipulative Sabrina's mother could be. I saw it but did not want to let Mia know what I knew. She would undoubtedly stop being as compassionate towards Efelia as she had been. I wasn't going to let her know what I had come to conclude. I could not tell her. Not yet.

◆   ◆   ◆

I very seldom can remember my dreams. When we were in Maui for Chloe and Malcolm's wedding, I surprised Mia, Suzanna and Delphine by narrating in its every detail a very intriguing dream I had the night before. Even before we started eating our breakfast I was sharing my dream with them:

"Under my left foot was a cat stuck to my sock and I was having some trouble removing it. The cat transformed into a mouse, and that too was difficult to remove. All of a sudden, I realized that if I simply removed the sock I could get rid of the pest that was stuck to my foot. I went outside on the veranda and took off the sock. But then, lots of tiny flying insects erupted all around me. In the dream I asked myself why I hadn't gone farther away from the house to remove the sock instead of removing it so close to the living area and having all these bugs around! That was it!"

Delphine was the first one to exclaim: "What an amazing dream, Jean-Paul! It is just perfect."

"Would you interpret it for me, please?"

"Well, the cat symbolizes something familiar, like a nice pet. But it's preventing you from moving ahead if it's stuck under your foot. You don't want to step on it. The left side represents something that's not right. It's the sinister aspect of things. In Latin, sinister means left, you know!"

"When you try to shake the cat off, the nice pet turns into a pest. Removing the sock brings a lot of annoyance, things that 'bug' you. Wanting to remove the sock away from the house would indicate that you are concerned about 'bugging' your family about this whole business of your Venezuelan family."

What a vivid dream and how symbolic of my present situation. Mia wanted to know if I saw the dream the same way Delphine saw it. To her it was a precursor to what she's been praying for: that I become aware of the fact that the familiar pet—Efelia—had turned into a pest and that it is time to shake it off, and detach myself from it!

Later that day, as we were swimming in the crystal clear waters of Ulua Beach, in Wailea, Delphine picked a sock from under her feet that had been brought to shore by the waves: "Hey, Jean-Paul, here is your sock! And it is a purple one!!! The sea has washed it. So it's not only clean but whatever negative energy it held has been transmuted; that is what the color purple means: transmutation! You have gotten rid of all the little bugs. Look, the sock is perfectly clean!"

We all burst out laughing, and commented on the surprising 'coincidence' between the dream of the night before and this purple sock delivered by the ocean. If what my dream indicated was true, it would not be long before my relationship with Mia became once again loving, passionate and trusting. I was ready for the transmutation!

I had wanted, for the sake of our little girl, to encourage the friendship between two women: one who is my life's companion, and the other the mother of my youngest daughter. They may dislike one another but I have ties with both of them. It will not be difficult to shake off the sock and get rid of all the little bugs. We will soon be leaving Venezuela.

◆   ◆   ◆

The day we returned to Caracas from Maui, Danielle called to say that she was in labor. I booked Mia on a flight to Austin that was leaving two days later and she went alone to visit our first grandson, the most gorgeous baby that ever was, London James the first!

Mia spent a couple of weeks with Danielle, Michael and Baby London and it was an occasion for me to enjoy Sabrina and her brother Sergio for a sleepover at the apartment. We had great fun together as we always do when they are with me. We spent hours at the pool, ate pizza, watched TV, played monopoly and Spanish scrabble, and had a grand time.

Suzanna flew in from Phoenix to catch the same plane that was bringing Mia back to Caracas after her visit to Austin. Our middle daughter wanted to vacation in Venezuela before starting her Masters program in Science and Technology the following month.

She has become a true inspiration to us these past few years: the books she has either recommended or given to us have been very instrumental in our spiritual growth and Mia told me that she expected nothing short of magical during her stay in Caracas as Suzi always manages to awaken something in our inner self.

For years, Mia and I have listened to recordings of philosophers, or authors such as Brian Tracy, Jim Rohn, Tony Robbins, Stephen Covey, and several others and we always encouraged our daughters when they were in their teenage years to use the time spent in the car as learning time. We had discovered that one of our favorite subjects was personal growth. Our daughters had followed in our footsteps and were avid readers of self-help books.

Suzanna was eager to share with us what new books she had recently bought: one was *Trust Your Vibes,* by Sonia Choquette. When she had seen her at a conference it made her think of Mia: she was happy and carefree!

We had a wonderful time with our daughter. We visited the German village of Colonia Tovar, where we had lunch. We also explored the pueblo of El Hatillo, discovered some unexplored areas of Caracas our efficient driver Miguel took us to. We enjoyed Japanese, Indian or Italian food at our favorite restaurants during her stay in Venezuela. Miguel knew his city well and was a perfect guide.

One morning, Mia asked Suzanna to act as mediator between the two of us, and with my permission, she asked our daughter to help us get through some issues regarding how I had been acting, especially these past couple of years. Another one of the books our daughter had bought for us was by Esther and Jerry Hicks and both Mia and Suzanna had commented how the book was answering many of the questions that troubled Mia. They were constantly referring to it and I made a note to one day read it too. The book was about the law of allowing. It was *Ask and It Is Given.*

Our Suzi listened attentively and remained as neutral as she could. We call her our little Buddha, because she has this beautiful, constant smile on her face. It reflects her inner calm, her sense of being in a good place, with little or no judgment. We knew we could rely on her fairness. She would listen to us and help us both see when we needed to yield. She would encourage her mother: "Trust your vibes, Mom, and keep the faith!"

Mia brought up the fact that one of the things she resented the most was my not apologizing for some of the most painful incidents between us.

"You made some of them sound so insignificant. That's really been hurtful."

I tried to give Mia a hug and she brushed me off. I did apologize for my lack of honesty and for the way I had been insensitive to her feelings.

"You know, darling. The reason why I didn't say I was sorry about the nail incident for example is really because it meant nothing to me. I didn't think I needed to apologize. But I understand now how it made you feel. And I'm really sorry."

I decided to share something with our daughter: "Did Mom tell you about Sabrina's birthday party?"

"No, what happened?"

"The mother decided to have it on our wedding anniversary."

Mia cut in: "And I wasn't invited!"

"What? Why?"

"She said it would be embarrassing for her to have me there. This is a woman I have invited in our home when Chloe and Malcolm were here at Christmas time. As if *that* was not embarrassing to me? Especially when your father wanted to sit next to her and her kids for a family picture, leaving me alone at the other end of the couch! I wanted to scream!"

"Oh no! What did you do?"

"I asked him to come and sit next to me. He got so mad, he yelled at me later, when we were alone and he accused me of not being able to accept the fact that Sabrina is his daughter, of being jealous of her … It wasn't your dad talking. It was a different man!"

"Wel, your mom couldn't let go. You know how she always wants things her way! I just wanted to sit next to my daughter!"

"We had a huge fight." Mia informed our daughter. "I had a meltdown and cried so much that day I thought it was over between your father and me. It was Christmas Day and it was ruined because of this. The damage was pretty massive. I needed help from my psychologist friend Beatriz to recover after that scene. I think that's when I asked each one of you girls if I could come for a visit. If I had a home elsewhere, I would have left this country. It took me several days to get over it, and I reassured myself with my 'This too shall pass' mantra. And I prayed a lot!"

"So, what happened with Sabrina's party? Did you go, Dad?"

"Of course not!" I replied. "And Efelia started screaming at me when I told her I wouldn't attend. She said that I was choosing to be with my wife instead of attending my daughter's birthday party, when I had celebrated 33 other anniversaries with your mom, and that it showed how little I cared about my daughter."

"And I had no idea! Your father kept this to himself for several days!"

"She knew very well that we had another invitation that day—a first communion—and that I was going there with your mom." I continued: "I told Efelia that she was extremely manipulative and that nothing that she did or said would make me change my mind and go to Sabrina's party. She was seething when I dropped her off after helping her with the piñata. I knew there and then that a bond had broken between us."

"You see, Suzita, your dad was always afraid of what Efelia could do to him if he didn't behave the way she wanted him to. We both knew how she could manipulate him. She had threatened him a few times to disappear from his life with his daughter. We never knew what it meant. Since her father had committed suicide, who knows what she could be insinuating? So, for your dad to tell her, finally: *¡Basta, ya!* (Enough, already!), that's big, that's huge! Unfortunately, your dad paid dearly for being so outspoken!"

"How is that?" Suzi wanted to know.

"The next two weekends, she prevented me from seeing Sabrina."

"What?"

"Yep! When I called, she said they were going somewhere. There are 3 days each weekend that I could see her: Friday evening, Saturday or Sunday. Two weekends in a row, not once, not for half a day, not for one hour. Nada. She would not let me see my daughter! I would call and leave messages. She would not even call back!"

"That's so sad that she would use Sabrina to get back at you, Dad!"

Mia wanted to know:

"Sometimes I ask myself: Why does she create such turmoil between your father and me? We were stuck in Caracas two weekends in a row when we could have gone to Los Roques or Merida! When Dad told me later about Sabrina's party and how she did not want me there, I wondered what I had done for her to be so spiteful."

"Mom, Dad chose you. That's what you've done! He chose to stay with you! That's all!"

"Hmm. Thanks, Sweetie. I guess that's it. But your father was misleading me because he wanted me to be nice to her. He'd tell me: 'She admires you so much!' So I'd make an effort to tolerate her, to accept her in our lives. Now you know what Dad says: 'You can admire someone even if you don't like the person.' I'm not sure about that!"

"I've always known that she was lying," I commented. "For stupid things mostly. She would lie to Sabrina and say: 'You're only going to visit for a few hours,' when in fact we had agreed that Sabrina was spending the night. So of course the kid would start crying when she'd find out she was staying over. And she was angry at me, not at the mother!"

"Aye, Daddy. *Quelle affaire!*"

"My concern is that she's teaching her daughter to lie or pretend" I said. "Sabrina can become physically ill just because she's upset about something. She once started having what seemed like an asthma attack: she was coughing, crying, choking. I had to take her back home! Of course when we got there, she was fine!"

Suzanna wanted to know: "So does the mother have a boyfriend?"

"Had. He's gone. Moved to Spain," I replied.

"Too bad. Maybe if she had a boyfriend …"

"She'd leave your father alone," Mia continued, "I thought so too. We were so happy when she was going out with a man from her office, but he moved away."

"So now that she knows that you know she's not who she pretended to be, she's acting differently?"

"Maybe she got tired of pretending. Or she finally came to the realization that I wasn't going to leave your mom for her. Who knows? Maybe she still had some hope. She calls less often."

Mia thanked Suzanna for the clarity that we were both getting from this family discussion. It was so important to Mia especially to be able to have someone on her side, who could hear her plea! It was helping me as well. I was made aware of how negatively the situation had affected our relationship.

Suddenly it dawned on me that trying to cover-up for Efelia in order to sustain harmony between all of us had not had the desired effect. It was essentially because of Sabrina that I wanted Mia and Efelia to be friends. I now could see how that might never happen.

21

The reconciliation

Before she left Caracas to return to Phoenix, Suzanna and I spoke about how confident we were that her dad would soon get rid of the guilt that was causing so much stress and also the somewhat obsessive behavior he displayed towards his youngest daughter. She reminded me to keep my focus on what I desired, not on what I feared might happen!

I consulted my Feng Shui books and did more cleansing of the energies in our apartment, lighting tea lights placed in a circle on my prayer table, ringing crystal bells, and praying to my angels and guides so they would bring back harmony into our lives. I sat in front of my healing altar and bathed myself in divine light. I was keeping the focus on what my heart desired. I would remain in this contemplative state until tears of gratitude would roll down my cheeks. I repeated to myself over and over:

"I live in a constant state of gratitude. I am blessed, I am so blessed!"

I felt truly grateful for the life I lived, for the love I felt in my heart, for the beautiful family God had blessed me with, for being loved so deeply by my husband and my wonderful daughters, for my excellent health, my high level of energy, for my caring friends, my new adorable grandbaby. Gratitude was replacing every other unhealthy emotion I still harbored. I was at peace, I felt confident that I would overcome these hurdles.

I found myself thinking about the work that had been necessary to help our marriage survive. My personal journals had been a source of great comfort. They truly were my best therapy. I kept three separate ones: one in which I recounted events in my life that either were troubling me or were worth recording; a prayer journal in which I listed the petitions brought to my healing table, and a gratitude journal listing at least five things I was thankful for each day. I didn't write every day in all three but whenever I was faced by a challenge, I would write a Dear God letter, thank the Mother/Father God for the last prayer answered and then write a new one. When I read back some of my petitions, I realized even more the amazing power of prayers. So many were answered. So many blessings were showered upon me!

A prayer I wrote stated: "Dear Father/Mother God, dear protective angels, please guide me and help me. Fill my heart with peace, love, joy, tolerance, wisdom, patience, gratitude, generosity, happiness."

Some of the things I was grateful for are listed in my gratitude journal:

The feeling of bliss, lightness and ecstasy while meditating

The laughter that brings out the tears

The calm after the storm

The romance we still create, the passion we still enjoy

The more appreciation was shown, the more blessings I seemed to be receiving. Another tool I used was my treasure map. A dear friend taught me many years ago how to make a collage with the things we'd like to attract into our life.

She recommended to have a written description as well as pictures of what we would like to achieve and add words expressing the desired outcome, where they could be seen daily. The wall behind my computer screen is where I hung my poster, my dreams' collage. Pictures of Jean-Paul and me are surrounded by images of places we'd like to visit and things we'd like in the next house we will be building. I added words that resonated with me: Faith, Trust, Resilience, Perseverance, Miracle, Joy, Courage, Healing! A vision board is a constant reminder of what the possibilities are. My life already reflected how powerful these manifestation boards could be: new ones were necessary every few years, after some of the dreams on the board were becoming reality.

When Jean-Paul and I were first going through the trials of his involvement with Efelia, I made smaller collages that I would give him when he'd come home after an overseas trip: pictures of the two of us at different stages of the relationship with images of places where we'd been together, and powerful messages such as this one: "A marriage is a constant work in progress, a truly lovely, loving work of heart!"

Some of these collages were like giant greeting cards, with the message and pictures inside, and I would leave them where he could see them, on his desk, inside our walk-in closet, or on his night table. I wanted these small vision boards to remind him of all the years spent together, and of the many magic moments we shared.

Another helpful exercise is found in a book by Ellen Kriedman, *Light His Fire*. She recommends writing on index cards tips on how to improve the relationship. This is what I wrote on my cards:

Tell Jean-Paul I'm glad he's part of my life, how lucky I am to have him.

Give him a compliment once a day, tell him how much he matters to me.

Listen with my heart, not with my head.

Touch him every day, a pat, a hug, hold hands, rub his back, kiss him.

Let go of worry.

Stand behind your feelings. Ask for what you want. Be honest in your communication. Tell him how you truly feel.

Make it safe for him to tell you the truth without becoming angry.

Be playful. Make a wish list (his and hers). Share what you wrote with each other.

I had brought my index cards with me to Caracas. I had done most of what was suggested at one time or another. My focus had really been on bettering our relationship. It hadn't been easy yet we were still together, we were still in love with one another!

◆   ◆   ◆

On the Friday following Suzanna's visit, my husband came home with a big smile on his face, squeezed me tightly in his arms, gave me a passionate kiss and invited me to one of the finest Italian restaurants in Caracas, Vizzio's.

I was puzzled: Jean-Paul's face was all lit up! He seemed to be years younger. He also looked like he'd been liberated!

"Wow, you are in a jolly mood, my love." I commented. "What's up?"

"Oh, nothing. The week went by quickly. The project is almost finished. We'll be leaving Caracas soon. Let's celebrate!"

"Yeah, and there's something else." I wanted to know. "You seem so different, so ... relieved!"

"I'm realizing a few things. I know it hasn't been easy for you to deal with the situation here in Venezuela. I guess I didn't want to admit it, but Efelia is really showing a different side."

"Hmm. Did something else happen?" I asked hesitantly.

"Would you believe that she's asking me for more money now?" Jean-Paul's reply surprised me.

"No! Really?" I was smiling, my curiosity aroused.

"I told her she'll have to show me receipts. I know she is worried because we're leaving soon. She asked me if I was going to abandon them."

"After all you've done for her," I commented, "I'm surprised she would think so poorly of you. She should be more appreciative!"

"I think she is but she's also worried that I may forget them."

"How could that possibly be?" I wondered aloud. "Although, since she isn't getting any support from Sergio's father, she may be worried that we might disappear from her life once we leave Venezuela. Imagine what it would be like for them if she didn't have you.

"I paused and Jean-Paul remained silent.

"You should remind her that she has a valuable apartment in her name!"

"I wanted my daughter to live in a better neighborhood." Jean-Paul replied. "The apartment is for Sabrina. I had made myself a promise that I would get them out of the barrio where they used to live. So I did!"

"Well, darling, that's a great accomplishment. Your daughter will thank you one day for this."

"I'm learning to detach myself from her, you know! London is helping me become less preoccupied with Sabrina. I'm so happy to finally have a little boy in our family."

I was happy to have our little London as well. Our first grandbaby was such a bundle of joy! He truly was a gift from heaven. He had come into our lives at the right time, when Jean-Paul needed something, someone to distract him from the obsessive attention he was giving Sabrina.

I wanted Jean-Paul to realize something:

"You know what I'm grateful for? That Sabrina was never very demonstrative toward us. Her lack of affection is helping us say goodbye. Imagine how we'd feel if she had been as expressive as our friends' kids who often jump in our arms when they see us. Sabrina probably protected herself by not being overly affectionate toward us, and hopefully it won't be too hard for her when we leave Venezuela."

"Maybe you're right." Jean-Paul admitted. "She's preparing herself for the separation."

"I must say that I often wondered why you were insisting on visiting with her every weekend that we were in Venezuela. Even our drivers would ask me: 'What will happen when you go back home? How will Sabrina feel?' I now see that you wanted to become a constant figure in her life because you only had a short time here in Caracas. You wanted to make sure she'd remember you. But me, since her birth, I had decided that I would not get attached to Sabrina because she could never be with us. We live in two different continents!"

"Well, Jean-Paul replied, I was also trying to reduce her attachment to the mother. The trips alone with her to Margarita Island and to Disney definitely helped me get closer to her!"

"I'm so happy that she's more comfortable with you now."

"It wasn't easy but there's been a big improvement!" Jean-Paul commented.

I wanted Jean-Paul to know:

"Aren't we lucky to have survived these past months, these past years? Seven years is a long time, and I never thought it would take that much work. But I can finally say that I am completely healed!"

"Wow! You really sound much better, darling." Jean-Paul commented. "I knew all along that you'd be able to survive these challenging times."

"My heart is smiling again and jumping in my chest with joy!" I told Jean-Paul excitedly. "I feel absolutely no anger or bitterness toward Efelia. I know what happened to me: I was insecure and fearful and I attracted more of what I feared! The more I thought about your attachment to them, the more you seemed to be attached. Frankly I feel sorry for Efelia. She was probably still in love with you all these years, and it must have been hard for her to observe our relationship so closely. I pray that she finds a man to love and marry. I wish she too could be happy. I feel so blessed that this is now all behind us. I am so happy I could burst!"

"I'm so glad to hear that! I love to see you happy!" Jean-Paul's entire face was smiling.

"I've also come to realize something," I confessed, "a lot of the upset of the past few years, I probably brought upon myself: I was living in fear and I was getting more of what I was fearing. I let doubt and worry take over too often. I'm very thankful to have overcome these trials."

"Some of your fears were unfounded." Jean-Paul wanted me to know. "Others I could see why you would experience them. I've known for some time who Efelia really is."

I was listening very attentively. Jean-Paul didn't speak too often about Efelia anymore. He knew I preferred not to bring her name inside our home. But he wanted to share something with me:

"I didn't want to tell you because of Sabrina. She's so sensitive that she might have felt a change in your attitude toward her mother if I confided in you. We will never know for sure, but even I had some doubts about whether or not the pregnancy was really an accident. But it's the past. We should just let it all go!"

It was the first time Jean-Paul was alluding to this since Sabrina's birth. He had denied any entrapment on her part, while I had always believed it was most probably the case. I would have liked to acknowledge the small victory I'd won: He was finally admitting that maybe she had played her cards very carefully ... But Jean-Paul had a good point: We should just let it go. I would not elaborate on his remark. He had a daughter he needed to be concerned about. She was an innocent consequence of his and Efelia's irresponsible behavior. She should not be the one to pay the price.

"You're right," I replied. "It doesn't matter anymore! We have our little London, an angel sent from heaven to help us get over the past, and that is the most wonderful gift we could have dreamed of! I remember wishing to have my own little baby to love and adore, only a few years ago. Maybe so you would experience firsthand how I felt when you showered Sabrina with so much attention. I guess I was a little jealous of the love you have for her. I yearned to give my unconditional love to my own little child. London is the closest thing to having my own baby. I get to enjoy him for a few days and then I give him back to his parents. It's so perfect to be a grandma!"

"A new stage in our lives." Jean-Paul commented.

"Aren't we blessed to experience it together?" I asked him. "Aren't you lucky I didn't give up on you?"

"I knew you wouldn't give up on me. Besides, I love you enough for both of us, and I knew that we would always be together."

"Do you know why you had such an obsession in your relationship with Sabrina?" I asked.

"I wanted to win her affection and I only had a few months to do it. I also wanted to help her become more independent of the mother," Jean-Paul admitted. "There's a huge difference between the girl we saw when we first arrived, and who she is today, right?"

"Huge difference indeed. She's a different child. It's been almost two years, you know!" I commented. "And it was a rocky road. I thought of moving to Maui."

I said it with a smile. Jean-Paul looked at me inquisitively:

"You wouldn't have left me here all by myself!" He was right: I probably would not have.

"Well I nearly did." I wanted him to know. I "When you asked me to go away so you could be alone with your daughter it felt as if you wanted us to separate. I was determined to patiently wait for you to get back to your senses. I must really love you, Baby!"

"I know you do, my love, and I love you more!"

I needed to confide in him:

"I think another reason why I stayed was because you make me laugh so much! I love how you can change my mood and take me from tears to laughter!"

"I'm glad!"

I was curious to know: "What do you think was the single most powerful element that helped us remain a couple?"

"Besides great sex?"

We both laughed. Jean-Paul hesitated only a few seconds. Then:

"Communication. Having this constant open dialogue in which we could both express our feelings without too much fear. It's good to be friends first. We can always count on our friendship. A friend forgives more easily than a spouse. I'm thankful that as friend, lover and spouse, we both had the heart to forgive."

Epilogue

In my journey of the past seven years, I could not have found the light at the end of the tunnel had it not been for the guidance of wonderful earthly angels put on my path to lead the way to peace, harmony and victory!

I knew there were several lessons we could learn from our trials. One of the important realizations I came to is that when we are in a negative mindset, all other negative misconceptions amassed during our lifetime surface to drag us down. Events in our lives that might seem innocuous enough on an ordinary day acquire a totally different light when we are steeped in negativity.

Nowadays, when I think of the mysterious illnesses that worried me for several months in Venezuela, I choose to believe that Jean-Paul having been there on several occasions before me would probably be immune to certain bacteria in the water. That would explain why I was the only one getting sick. I will never know for sure what really caused the sudden attacks that clobbered me on and off during these past several years, however. The last occurrence was when I had become terribly sick in the middle of the night while visiting my newborn grandbaby in Austin. The old fears resurfaced: I thought I was being attacked again! This line of thinking would only make things worse. Instead, I became conscious of my responsibility to care for and protect my grandbaby. I made a decision to completely reject the theory of evil curses. They obviously didn't survive my own attitude shift, which was to be ever so vigilant of my thoughts and to surrender to the divine force. Once I stopped giving the symptoms fuel, they simply evaporated into thin air.

As I became aware of my own human frailty, I saw my relationship with others like a mirror that was reflecting back to me my own image! I learned to accept myself as I am, entirely, without trying to repress or suppress feelings that I deemed unworthy. By expressing non-judgment, it reflected directly on my relationships. I experienced a release and a movement forward when I stopped desiring to project the idea of the perfect wife. I was able to give the people around me space to grow and the opportunity to experience their own life, respecting where they stand now and supporting them with love on their personal paths.

There was a time not too long ago, when it was unsettling for me to have a picture of Sabrina in display in our home. I had bought an album, which I had filled with her pictures for Jean-Paul. I could not bring myself to put it in a place where I could see it daily. It stirred a dormant sadness and I simply put away framed pictures and photo albums of Jean-Paul's other family where only he could see them, inside his walk-in-closet, his desk or his night table. Out of sight, I wasn't reminded as often of their existence.

When we moved to our Houston apartment after we were repatriated from Caracas, I put two framed pictures of his little girl on Jean-Paul's desk in the office he and I share at home. It makes me smile when I look at one picture in particular. When I first showed it to Jean-Paul, he thought it was our Suzanna when she was five years-old. And he commented:

"Doesn't she remind you of Sabrina?"

I thought he was joking, so I replied:

"No, not at all!"

He looked more carefully, and rephrased the question:

"You don't think she looks like Sabrina?"

Then I said: "Honey, it is Sabrina! This is the bicycle you bought for her three years ago. You don't recognize her?"

It is true that in that particular picture, there is an uncanny resemblance with Suzanna when she was the same age. I can feel the change in my heart, my complete acceptance for the child I had promised myself I would love because she was my husband's. My heart has finally healed. Sabrina's pictures no longer trigger any bitterness. Her smiling face near the computer screen on Jean-Paul's desk shows me a happy girl who is now part of my life.

Jean-Paul has demonstrated to me that when he made the decision to end his involvement with Efelia, he kept his word. He no longer harbored deep feelings for her. When he kept information about their friendship from me, it was because he sensed that their closeness would bother me. He finally understood that the hiding of the truth was really what I despised the most. Once reassured that he could tell me anything at all, the openness in our conversations took a different turn.

When I asked myself why I had been infuriated by Jean-Paul's lack of honesty, I realized that it stemmed from my need to always control his every action, especially those concerning his relationship with Efelia. No wonder he had preferred to lie rather than face my fury when he took her out to lunch or when he was at their apartment longer than he would admit. I had been temperamental, with my "captain of the world" attitude as he calls it! A natural shift occurred when I told Jean-Paul he could spend as much time with his daughter as he wished. It no longer bothered me. I felt confident that their looking like a family from which I was excluded took nothing away from my relationship with my husband. Efelia had not had an easy life. She was going to have to care for her two children as a single mother. It was only normal that she would continue to seek and depend on our support.

The apparent manipulation that caused so many conflicts in our marriage altered the image Jean-Paul had of Efelia. And we both agreed that, having been abandoned by the father of her son, it was hard for her to believe that Jean-Paul wouldn't do the same thing. She used his attachment to his daughter to manipulate him because that was the only tool she had.

When we went to say goodbye, on the way to the airport, Jean-Paul and I both gave Efelia a kiss on the cheek. I hadn't seen her in months, and I barely recognized her when she met us in front of their apartment building. She had highlighted her hair and it was almost blond. She was wearing a strapless top and very tight jeans. We both exclaimed: "WOWWWW!" She was all made up, had new black-framed eyeglasses that were quite stylish. She looked the best I had ever seen her. And she seemed happy! Both Jean-Paul and I were at the same time surprised and relieved at the new Efelia we saw that morning we bid them farewell. Even our conductor Miguel noticed the transformation. Saying goodbye was not sad at all. I made no attempt to kiss Sabrina since she started running away from us as soon as Jean-Paul himself tried. I knew that she would come to terms one day with the situation, and that when she's older, she'll understand who I am and why I am in her life.

Having the heart to forgive is the reason why Jean-Paul and I are together today. Forgiveness brings solace to the mind. It is soothing, it is cleansing, and it is healing. What Jean-Paul and I have between us is precious. If we were asked why our relationship survived, and how we can still experience the vibrancy, the passion and the deep love we enjoy today, it could be summed up in one word: forgiveness.

We are both infused with renewed enthusiasm about life and we are in a constant state of expectation about what our future has in store. We breathe easier, we laugh more whole-heartedly and we talk less hesitantly about our feelings for one another.

We are focusing on our dreams, watching them manifest one by one, and creating new ones every day. Life is a wondrous, marvelous, adventurous roller-coaster ride and we are enjoying every moment, respecting and trusting enough to give each other the space to grow.

As a very dear friend once wrote to me, the heart that forgives is a heart that embraces all and fills up with unconditional love. It is a heart expanded that resonates to feel the pain of others as its own pain. Their joy is its joy. It is a heart that embraces all human frailties as its own, a heart willing to change and grow to allow divine love to flow. It is an on-going process that is not without its aches and pains. The rewards, however, are beyond compare!

The End

RECOMMENDED MATERIAL

BOOKS

Chopra, Deepak. *The Path to Love—Spiritual Strategies for Healing,* Harmony Books, 1997—Three Rivers Press, 1997

Covey, Stephen R.—*The 7 Habits of Highly Effective People,* Simon and Shuster, NY, 1989

De Angelis, Barbara—*Secrets about Life Every Woman Should Know*—Ten principles for Total Emotional and Spiritual Fulfillment, Hyperion, NY, 1999

Dyer, Wayne W.—*There's a Spiritual Solution to Every Problem,* HarperCollins, NY, 2001

Gray, John—*How to Get What You Want and Want What You Have,* HarperCollins, NY, 1999

Hicks, Esther, Jerry—*Ask and it is Given—Learning to Manifest Your Desires,* Hay House, 2004

Rohn, Jim—*Leading an Inspired Life,* Jim Rohn International, TX, 1997

Williamson, Marianne—*A Return to Love,* HarperCollins, NY, 1992

AUDIO RECORDINGS

Dyer, Wayne W.—*Power of Intention,* Hay House
www.hayhouse.com

Robbins, Anthony—*The time of Your Life*, Robbins Research Int'l, www.Tonyrobbins.com

Rohn, Jim, *Cultivating an Unshakable Character*, Jim Rohn Int'l, Southlake,TX, www.JimRohn.com

Tracy, Brian—*The Psychology of Achievement*, Nightingale Conant, www.Nightingale.com

LIVE CONFERENCES, SEMINARS, WORKSHOPS

Date with Destiny—Anthony Robbins—a transformational seminar over 5 1/2 days in which you discover your life purpose, after identifying your core values and the beliefs that shape your destiny and influence your decisions. www.Tonyrobbins.com

Hay House I-Can-Do-It Conference—a gathering of several of the most inspiring spiritual leaders of our time www.hayhouse.com

MEDITATION PRACTICE

Guided Meditation by John Gray, www.marsvenus.com

Twin Hearts Meditation, www.pranichealing.com

*For additional copies
of this book
visit the author's website at
www.thehappiestwoman.net or
call 281-466-4085*

978-0-595-44286-7
0-595-44286-2

Printed in the United States
108345LV00005B/1-141/P